Heroes and Villains

Heroes and Villains

MIKE ALSFORD

BAYLOR UNIVERSITY PRESS

First published in 2006 by
Darton, Longman and Todd Ltd
1 Spencer Court
140–142 Wandsworth High Street
London SW18 4JJ

Published in USA by
Baylor University Press
One Bear Place #97363
Waco, TX 76798
Texas, USA

Designed and produced by Sandie Boccacci
Phototypeset in 11/12pt Bembo
Cover design by Judy Linard

Library of Congress Cataloging-in-Publication Data

Alsford, Mike
  Heroes and villains / Mike Alsford.
    p. cm.
  Includes bibliographical references and index.
  ISBN-13: 978-1-932792-92-8 (pbk.: alk. paper)
  1. Heroes in mass media. 2. Villains in mass media. 3. Mass media—
Moral and ethical aspects.
  I. Title.
  P96.H46A46 2006
  302.2308—dc22

                                                                2006032549

Printed and bound in Great Britain

For Lauren and Amy
who tend to bring out the hero in me.

Huge thanks to
Grace and 'The Ginger Twins' Sarah and Claire
for reading over the manuscript
'just one more time please!'
You all went above and beyond,
you rock!

Contents

Preface

Elsewhere I have spoken of creating an *interdisciplinary explora-tory space* within which to raise and discuss a variety of issues relating to the human condition.[1] In this book I am committed to the same endeavour. What I mean by this is that I am concerned here to create an arena for raising issues, stimulating debates and introducing a range of ideas and thinkers. While my own opinions will inevitably come through – that can never be avoided – I hope that readers will feel that they are part of an exploration rather than simply the recipients of a body of knowledge.

It has become something of a commonplace within our increasingly postmodern culture to assert the elusiveness of absolutes not least any absolute notion of what constitutes human being. The anti-humanist tradition initiated by Nietzsche, and brought into sharper focus by thinkers such as Martin Heidegger and Michel Foucault, speaks of the inability of humanity to look itself in the face, that is to be able to study itself in a disinterested manner.

> all human sciences advance towards the unconscious only with their back to it.[2]

And again:

> to all those ... who refuse to think without immediately thinking that it is man who is thinking, to all these warped and twisted forms of reflection we can answer only with a philosophical laugh – which means, to a certain extent, a silent one.[3]

However far one wishes to go with Foucault in this it seems

beyond doubt that as human beings we are as incapable of considering ourselves dispassionately and objectively as we are anything else in the world, and quite possibly even more so. The gift of self-knowledge is a rare one indeed and even the ability to see ourselves as others see us is an elusive one.

What we are and what it is that drives us represents a lifelong quest for both the individual human being and humanity as a whole. Whether or not one takes a naturalistic, a metaphysical or religious perspective on human identity, whether or not one favours an essentialist or existential stance on the nature of human existence what it is to be human remains a mystery to us. Try asking yourself 'Who and what am I?' and you will see what I mean.

While there are many valuable and insightful things that may be said about being human none of them ever comes close to exhausting the subject. While we are driven to explore ourselves in the arts and sciences, through work and play, through the way we engage with others and through introspection and reflection we may never account for ourselves without remainder. Even those who have committed themselves to a religious worldview, such as Christianity, are not a great deal better off in this regard. The big theological symbols such as the *image of God* or the *soul* or *spirit* are far too nebulous to provide us with anything other than generalities – however significant these might be.

Paradoxically the establishing of what it means to be human is both necessary and fraught with danger. It is necessary if we wish to establish, however vaguely, what is an appropriate mode of behaviour both from and towards a human being. In short, it is difficult to decry the behaviour of others as inhuman or as contravening human rights if we don't have some idea of what the term human actually means. On the other hand, too precise a definition of humanness, as we have learned to our cost, very easily gives way to notions of genetic purity, ethnic cleansing, slavery and genocide.

All this having been said, what I propose to do is to explore the notion of humanness in a tangential way by considering how we understand the twin notions of hero and villain particularly as they are portrayed in contemporary media. As mentioned above, what I am about here is creating an exploratory space, an arena where issues concerning humanness can be considered from a perhaps unfamiliar angle. I am equally concerned that this space should be an interdisciplinary one, one in which the issues are raised by familiar cultural images but may be commented on from a variety of viewpoints.

While trying to introduce the subject of *otherness* or *power*, for example, is a sure fire way of getting one crossed off party lists and ignored in pubs, talking about the latest *Spiderman* or *X-Men* film or the merits of *Buffy the Vampire Slayer* generally manages to generate a rather stimulating debate.

It has been my experience that raising primal questions through the use of familiar media images serves to demystify important debates often regarded as the sole preserve of the expert academic. While someone untrained in the fields of philosophy or theology, for example, may balk at commenting upon deontological versus teleological ethics they may have plenty to say concerning the relative behaviours of the Batman and Superman.

I have chosen my examples of the heroic and the villainous largely from contemporary imaginative sources rather than draw upon the wealth of classical material that covers similar ground. My reasons for this are simple, I want, as far as possible to allow as many to join in the debate as possible – not only those with a classical education. In drawing upon current heroic and villainous characters from sources such as *The Lord of the Rings*, *Buffy the Vampire Slayer*, the *Harry Potter* novels and a host of comic book figures such as The Batman and Spiderman I hope to be deploying examples that are familiar to the widest possible audience and that have a broad popular appeal.

Throughout the course of this book we shall be considering the importance of the imagination as a source of insight into the human condition then move on to explore ideas such as otherness, power and villainy. I believe that what establishes someone as a hero or a villain and, more importantly perhaps, what prompts us to define a person in either of these ways, can provide us with a useful insight into the values we consider important in any definition of what it means to be human. Let's see if I'm right shall we?

1

Myth and Imagination

I'm not making any promises ...

Call it a weakness if you like but as a general rule I don't like to disappoint people. That is certainly not to say that I never ever do, but I don't like either the look of sad dismay or bitter betrayal that tends to accompany a serious 'letting down', whether it is from students to whom I had promised a sizzling rollercoaster of a course of study, which turns out instead to be a shopping list of dead thinkers, or from my young daughter who I promised to allow to use me for target practice just as soon as I finished one last thing, or from friends whom I always promise to visit or from family members to whom I occasionally make all manner of rash and invariably unfulfilled DIY-related promises. It probably has something to do with wanting to be popular. I don't like complaining in shops either. With this in mind I most certainly don't want to disappoint or 'let down' those of you kind enough to be reading this book – even those of my students who are doing so out of loyalty or simply to 'suck-up'. So it makes sense for me to try to explain what I am about here, why I am doing what I am doing and in what way, while trying not to make any wild and unguarded promises about what this book may or may not do for you. I am quite postmodern enough to side-step these issues with the useful claim that you are at liberty to make of the text what you will. The book is entitled *Heroes and Villains* and so you can at least be reasonably assured that we will be encountering examples of the heroic and the villainous throughout its pages, but in what ways and why?

I have been a fan of heroic fiction in a variety of forms for as long as I can remember, whether it was Robin Hood storming Nottingham castle with a smile on his face, a sword in one hand and maid Marion tucked neatly under one arm, or Luke Skywalker invading the Death Star with a smile on his face, a light saber in one hand and Princess Leia tucked neatly under one arm, or Spiderman invading the lair of Dr Octopus with a smile under his mask, a web shooter on his wrist and Mary Jane Watson tucked neatly under one arm. Now while this might say a great deal about my own preoccupation with weapons and women, images of the hero and their villainous counterparts have, in my view, served as iconic receptacles for a wide range of cultural values, aspirations and fears. What a culture considers heroic and what it considers villainous says a lot about that culture's underlying attitudes – attitudes that many of us may be unaware that we have, and which represent cultural currents that we may be equally unaware of being caught up in. Take the three examples given above, Robin Hood, Luke Skywalker and Spiderman. The obvious point to be made about this group of heroes is that they are all men exhibiting a certain kind of aggressive power while their female companions are largely passive. Now while there have indeed been instances of heroic female characters throughout literature, I would suggest that it is only since the early 1980s that they have taken on a more active primary role in contemporary popular culture with figures such as Ellen Ripley (the *Aliens* films); Sarah Conner (the first two *Terminator* movies); Lara Croft (the *Tomb Raider* games); Xena, (*Xena: Warrior Princess*) and of course Buffy Summers (the *Buffy the Vampire Slayer* TV show). Now why should that be?

What I hope to do throughout this book is to explore the notions of hero and villain as portrayed in popular fiction so as to stimulate discussion concerning our contemporary values and attitudes, and the principles with which we navigate our way through life – what I shall refer to as our existential map. That heroic fiction is a useful way to approach this concern and to catalyse debate and discussion can be justified on the basis of the profound attraction humanity has always exhibited towards heroic and villainous figures, both real and imagined. The current success of films based on comic superheroes such as Spiderman and the X-Men, the revival of interest in heroic fantasy with the successful translation to film of Tolkien's *Lord Of The Rings, Xena: Warrior Princess,* the *Harry Potter* and *Buffy the Vampire Slayer* franchises all speak of this fascination with heroes and villains who navigate their way through the world based upon an absolute value system made manifest via an exercise of power. The confidence and certainty with which these figures apparently make their way through life is enviable particularly to ordinary human beings who, as a rule, tend to find themselves lost in a world of increasing complexity. It seems to me that the myth of the hero, and indeed the villain, represents our desire for a greater sense of confidence, personal identity and power to affect the world in which we find ourselves, through no fault of our own. Joseph Campbell in his classic work on heroes and mythology *The Hero With A Thousand Faces* makes this point:

> It has always been the prime function of mythology and rite to supply the symbols that carry the human spirit forward, in counteraction to those other constant human fantasies that tend to tie it back. In fact, it may well be that the very high incidence of neuroticism among ourselves follows from the decline among us of such effective spiritual aid.[1]

Campbell, drawing as he does upon the work of the psycho-analyst Carl Jung, argues that the myth of the hero confronts us with the challenge of transformation, the call to develop, to progress, to grow up by freeing ourselves form the limitations of infancy. Plotting a course through life requires heroic bravery, as the world can seem at best indifferent and at worst actively hostile to us. We need tools to guide us, although, as Campbell observes in the myth of Theseus's encounter with the monstrous Minotaur in the labyrinth, they might be simple ones:

> Adriane, the daughter of King Minos, fell in love with the handsome Theseus … [and] turned for help … to the crafty

Daedalus, by whose art the labyrinth had been constructed
… Daedalus simply presented her with a skein of linen
thread, which the visiting hero might fix to the entrance and
unwind as he went into the maze. It is, indeed, very little
that we need! But lacking that, the adventure into the
labyrinth is without hope.[2]

What I intend to do in the rest of this chapter is two things.
Firstly, to discuss the significance of establishing a mode of
behaviour in the world. Both hero and villain are often characterised as those who have a very clear agenda and system of
values. Where do we gain our perspective on the world? How do
we decide how to live in it? What are our reference points?
Secondly, in drawing primarily on fictional heroes and villains to
stimulate these discussions, we are making a sizeable claim for
the relevance of the imagination in exploring the human condition. For this reason we will spend some time outlining the
importance of the imagination and its products, and considering
what its key supporters and detractors have had to say.

Reference points and existential maps

In my experience – which I hesitate to absolutise – there are two
points in our lives when the crushing complexity of existence
comes into sharp focus, these are our mid-teens when we ask
such questions as 'Who am I and what the blazes am I going to
do with my life?' and our early forties where we ask the
questions 'Is this all I am and what the blazes have I done with
my life?' During these times we seek anchor points, points of
reference which might allow us to navigate, with some
semblance of intention and confidence, towards some clearly
perceived goals. These anchor points provide us with a sense of
structure to our lives by helping to establish order and meaning
and sense to our existence.[3] By order, I have in mind some notion
of consistency, the belief that there is pattern and regularity to
reality. A belief in order and routine, no matter how dull these
words might initially sound, is essential to human existence.
While chaos and disorder might very well be fun and stimulating
to entertain once in a while – wild parties, holiday impulses, mad

passionate love, for example – it would be next to impossible to live our lives with them around for too long. As Dr Seuss teaches us all too well, a visit from the *Cat in the Hat* begins to lose its appeal when he starts juggling with your goldfish. At the end of the day we like to know that certain things in our lives can be relied upon, that certain actions will produce predictable results and that the trains will run on time.

The quest for meaning is equally significant to our existence, the sheer fact of a thing is seldom sufficient for us. That a thing *is* is rarely as important as *why* a thing is. Even very young children do not put up with 'just because' for long, they very quickly want to know 'why?' The meanings and significances of objects in the world, both personal and impersonal, consume a great deal of our time. Aristotle famously maintained at the start of his *Metaphysics* that 'All men by nature desire to know'.[4] He goes on to argue that the highest manifestation of knowledge is wisdom, that is to say, the quest for knowledge concerning the cause of all things, what lies behind our immediate sense experience of the world. The interpretation of the world in which we find ourselves is the never-ending occupation of every human being, and the choice of tools we use to conduct this search for meaning is amongst the most important decisions we ever make. A world poorly understood is a world in which we are easily manipulated and a life without meaning is a poor thing indeed and one that is easily exploited.

Even the most disorganised of us – and I speak from experience here – are confounded by senselessness. We like things to make sense, to have purpose. In spite of our alleged move towards the postmodern where relativity and subjectivity are prioritised over the modernist celebration of absolutism and objectivity we still wrinkle up our noses, narrow our eyes and look generally put out when things or people 'don't make sense'. I suspect that Job in the Hebrew scriptures had exactly that look on his face while he was trying to figure out why God was being so nasty to him. All his friends kept assuring him that his sufferings only made sense if he had sinned and upset God in some way so it follows that he must have done. Job, I imagine, with his nose suitably wrinkled and his eyes narrowed to slits maintains that he had been a righteous man all his life and thus none of this makes any sense: 'If I have sinned, what have I done to you, O watcher of men? Why have you made me your target?'[5] Indeed Bildad, one of Job's now proverbial comforters, expresses similar confusion but where Job is confused over the apparent sense-lessness of Yahweh's attack upon him, Bildad is confused and suspicious over Job's claim to innocence: 'Surely God does not reject a blameless man or strengthen the hands of evildoers.'[6]

We like to believe there is a reason for everything, that even awful stuff like war and child abuse can be explained in some way. The senseless act doesn't simply anger us, it outrages us as it leaves us powerless and helpless to predict and plan for it, to respond to it in any meaningful way or indeed to protect against it. As we shall see later, so loathe are we to admit to our capacity for senseless acts we look for scapegoats to explain such acts in an attempt to get ourselves and humanity 'off the hook'.[7]

As we suggested earlier, to navigate our way through our existence – an existence that the philosopher Martin Heidegger teaches us is un-negotiated, one that we are just thrown into as it were – we require reference points, ideas, convictions and beliefs that we can anchor ourselves to in our quest for order and mean-ing and sense. Religions, ideologies, people and activities often serve to provide us with a kind of existential map, an overlay of principles, values and priorities which allow us to make judge-ments concerning the direction that our lives should take. Having such an existential map is not actually a matter of choice, only the nature of the map, where it is derived from and its reliability, are ever really at issue. To negotiate our way through life we are forced into the position of interpreting the world and the things we find in it, we are forced into making judgements and choices concerning the directions we wish to take – do I live here or there? Do I make friends with you or not? Do I have a family? Do I support or condemn this person or this action? Do I eat this, say that, wear the other? All of these decisions require points of reference which can either be arbitrarily assimilated via a passive, almost unconscious encounter with our immediate culture, or can be actively incorporated into our lives as an act of will.

One may choose, for example, to put oneself through the apparently arduous process of training to become a physio-therapist. However the the reasons for doing so will vary widely from person to person, depending upon the kind of reference points which make up one's existential map. If one has a set of values that prioritises others, considers human beings, even strangers, to be of value then the choice of a therapeutic career may well be stimulated by this. If one is principally concerned with material well-being then a career in physiotherapy might well be seen as a sound investment of one's time and energies. However, one might pursue such a course of training simply as a result of seeing someone on the TV shows *ER* or *Holby City* doing it, or because one's parents suggested it or because a friend did it. I sometimes wonder how many people signed up for courses in archaeology during the 1980s when the *Indiana Jones* films were first released. The sad truth is that we often make life-altering decisions on the basis of dubious and random collections of reference points and prevailing cultural trends.

To be able to ask such questions as 'Is this right?' or 'Is this good?' about anything, we need to invest these terms with mean-ing and significance. The question 'Is it right or good to be a soldier?' for example, requires a consideration of issues such as right for who? and good for what? Plato argued that the good life – a key theme in classical Greek philosophy – was one in which each individual knew their place in the social scheme of things. While this has very dubious implications, not least of which is the potential for social oppression, there is nevertheless a point here. A disengaged life of isolation where one never really feels part of the larger world and never truly feels that one is making a satisfying contribution to the human condition – no matter how small – is not an attractive prospect. As we shall see, while the hero often feels in some way alienated from the world by virtue of their special abilities or calling – Buffy is an excellent example of this – this is compensated for by their feelings of responsibility towards it and their sense of what I like to call *coadunacy* that is a heightened experience of the necessary interconnectedness and interdependency of humanity.

In many ways the hero helps to raise questions about the kind of decision we have to face and the values that might guide us. Heroes such as Buffy may have a great deal to teach us about our connectedness to the world and the implications of the choices we make.

Imagination

At this point I feel obliged to warn anyone who has read this far – and thank you for that – that what follows next is rather more demanding than what has come so far. I will explain why.

Nearly all of the heroic and villainous figures we will consider in this book will be drawn from the contemporary imagination for two basic reasons. First of all it is, I believe, in the imagination that we encounter heroes and villains in their most idealised form representing our purest heroic ideals and villainous fears. Secondly, by drawing our examples principally from contemporary imaginative products such as modern novels, TV and film, I hope to provide the non-specialist with an easy route into a discussion of the issues and themes relating to heroes and villains.

It is clearly the case that the hero and the villain have fought their eternal battle across all of human history and imagination. Myths and legends down the ages have told stories of those who fought for good or evil. History is full of instances of heroism and villainy in every field of human endeavour – artists, explorers, scholars, saints and martyrs, for example, have all helped to reveal to us the meaning of heroism. Similarly despots, tyrants, sociopaths and criminals have shown us the depths to which humanity can plummet. All this having been acknowledged, it is still the case that while relatively few people will have a classical education or a detailed knowledge of history, one would have had to be living in a very remote and isolated location for many years to have avoided some knowledge of *Lord of the Rings*, *Buffy* or *Superman*. So, addressing the second point above, contemporary examples from popular culture give us an attractive and accessible starting point.

Addressing the first point may be more complex – why the imaginative rather than real-life heroes and villains?

The importance of a varied and indeed imaginative perspective on familiar themes and issues is, I believe, an important one. To see ourselves as others see us has long been held a valuable if often salutary experience. To be surprised, even shocked by an encounter with the world is often a moment of existential, character-transforming significance. It is also an exercise of the imagination. As we shall see in subsequent chapters often the identification of a hero or villain is simply a matter of looking at someone in a different way.

The existentialist philosopher Karl Jaspers (1883–1969) talks about these shocking moments of encounter with the world as 'boundary experiences', moments in which our experience of order and meaning and sense is threatened, usually by extreme danger of some kind – death or the fear of death being the ultimate example of this. More often than not we live our lives according to carefully established routines. We act, think and emotionally engage in predictable and, for the most part, controlled ways. We walk to work the same way every day, we generally maintain the same opinions and values for most of our adult lives, and we even demonstrate the same emotional responses to stimuli such as loved ones and enemies. However, argues Jaspers, there are times when the carefully cultivated and regulated pattern of our life is upset by an encounter with something so extreme and unavoidable that only a transformation of our existence or an act of self-negating denial is possible. As we shall go on to see, it seems to me that the transformation of ourselves in response to boundary experiences of the world represents the truly heroic act,[8] while its denial speaks of an egocentricity which seeks to force the world to form around us. And as we know, world domination has always been the goal *par excellence* of the villain.

This process of encounter, challenge and transformation was described by the idealist philosopher Georg W.F. Hegel (1770–1831) as the process of dialectic – popularised as the relationship between thesis, antithesis and synthesis. According to Hegel the whole of reality is governed by the logic of this dialectic where something (the thesis) encounters its opposite (the antithesis) and, as a result of the ensuing conflict, a superior synthesis is achieved which then goes on to become a new thesis, and thus the process begins again. To encounter the alienness of the world, the otherness of the people that inhabit it, and the surprising often disconcerting facets of our own existence, requires both imagination, so as to perceive the potential for synthesis, and heroic resolve, such that we are prepared to leap into the unknown, to sacrifice what we are for what we may become.[9]

As Campbell suggests, heroes and villains can present us with the challenge to transformation, possibly enabling us to see ourselves and others in a new light. The heroes and villains continually thrown up by human imagination can be seen as powerful prototypes representing the extremes of human response to boundary situations.

So why the warning about the demands of the next section of this chapter? Various thinkers have argued that the imagination is a perfectly good and valid tool to use in gaining an insight into the nature of the world and the things we find in it. However, the value of the human imagination has not always been universally acknowledged, as we shall see.

Imagination and imagery have always played an important part within religions such as Christianity, Islam and Hinduism, whether this has been properly acknowledged or not, and heroic and even villainous images, as we shall see, often derive at least some of their substance from a messianic template. Furthermore, the images generated by religion have a habit of leaking over into secular life and culture. These images are understood to trigger a particular imaginative response in those encountering them.

The medieval Christian mythos, for example, has been a constant source of imagery for film makers, storytellers and artists of all kinds right up to the present day. While such classical works as Michelangelo's statue of *David* and the ceiling of the Sistine Chapel, Da Vinci's painting of the *Last Supper* and Handel's *The Messiah*, are intended as religious pieces for a religious audience many contemporary uses of religious imagery are not produced by religious people nor are they aimed at the religious. Heavenly choirs, crosses, people in robes, clouds, disembodied voices and gothic buildings make frequent appearances in films, advertisements, computer games and TV programmes.

What we shall do next, by way of preparation for a consideration of heroic and villainous images is to consider why imagery and imagination have, paradoxically, been viewed with, on the one hand, suspicion, and, on the other hand, as having a unique value within our culture.

The decline of the imagination

Classical literature as well as religious texts such as the Jewish scriptures, exhibited a considerable respect for the imagination as a legitimate means for the exploration and transmission of truths about the world and our place in it. Poetry, mythology, story and song were deployed as meaningful ways of describing the world in which we found ourselves and were considered particularly relevant as a means of illuminating the mysterious, be that the human psyche or the gods themselves. Examples of this can be found in the Egyptian myths of the gods of Heliopolis – particularly the family of Osiris; the Assyro-Babylonian creation myths and the epic of Gilgamesh; the Hebrew creation stories in the book of Genesis along with the poetic material found in the Song of Songs and the Psalms; the stories concerning the Greek Olympian pantheon; and tales of Celtic gods and heroes such as the *Tuatha De Danann* and *Cu Chulainn* from the Ulster Cycle, as well as many others. All of these mythic stories represent imaginative responses to primal questions concerning human origins and destiny along with foundational questions relating to the very nature and value of things. The origin of evil, and the struggle between it and its opposite, features large in many of these mythic cycles and as such the hero – whether god, demi-god or human agent of the gods is a common figure. That the world could be explored and indeed understood in this imaginative mode was beyond question by those who produced such tales. That stories were a legitimate and valuable way of engaging with fundamental existential and cosmological issues was taken for granted.

It was the period known as the Enlightenment which cast the greatest doubt upon the relevance of imagination as a means of exploring the truth about reality. We will therefore now consider how and why a range of thinkers contributed to the overall suspicion with which the imagination has been viewed within western culture particularly, but not exclusively, since the Enlightenment. To do this I will be introducing philosophers such as Plato, Descartes and Kant, all of whom sought to establish an absolute and primarily rational perspective on the world, implicitly (at least) throwing doubt on the role and value of imagination.

The quest for certainty

It seems to me that our culture has developed a level of dysfunction with regard to our need for variety and difference. While at one level we desire change, surprise, excitement and all of those things which allow us to experience the world with renewed wonder, we also fear change. We are fiercely protective of our routines, our individuality, our particular window on the world. This is by no means surprising. Even the greatest of philosophers, those whose thought helped to shape the culture we operate in could be said to have been motivated, at least in part, by fear of change and the chaos and instability that this may bring.

Plato (*c.* 428–348 BC), arguably the most famous and influential philosopher who ever lived, sought to establish the notion of a universe founded upon unchanging absolutes, what he called *Ideas* or *Forms*. Part of his motivation for this was to counter the subjective and rather negative teachings of the so-called Sophists – the name given to a loose grouping of popular travelling teachers. These Sophists opted, in the main, for a pragmatic approach to existence, one which rejected any notion of cosmic absolutes in favour of a sceptical and relativistic approach to life and truth. Plato was well aware of the destructive potential of the Sophist's teachings and thus taught that while the world that we perceive with our senses may very well be shadowy and ultimately unreal, it is founded upon an eternal and absolute blueprint. It is these absolutes that give us the confidence to speak of truth and beauty and justice, to work towards an ideal society and the good life.

Then it is an ideal pattern we were looking for when we tried to say what justice and injustice are in themselves, and to describe what justice and injustice are in themselves, and to describe what the perfectly just or perfectly unjust man would be like if he ever existed. By turning our eyes to them and seeing what measure of happiness or its opposite they would enjoy, we would be forced to admit that the nearer we approximate to them the more nearly we share their lot.[10]

In Book 7 of *The Republic* Plato develops his case by way of an analogy, the famous analogy of the cave. Imagine a cave in which people have been chained, facing the wall, since birth. For them, argues Plato, the world is made up of the shadows cast onto the cave walls by objects passing across some unseen fire light, 'in every way they would believe that the shadows of the objects we mentioned were the whole truth'.[11] Now consider what would happen if one of these cave dwellers were released and permitted first to turn and gaze upon the fire itself and then ultimately be guided out of the cave and into the sunlight. After a period of confusion and reorientation the freed prisoner would begin to encounter the real world, to see real objects and even to gaze upon the sun and finally 'he would come to the conclusion that it is the sun that produces the changing seasons and years and controls everything in the visible world, and is in a sense responsible for everything that he and his fellow-prisoners used to see.'[12] Of course when this newly enlightened person who sees the real world rather than the shadows returns to liberate his fellow prisoners he is treated with fear and suspicion and 'they would kill him if they could lay hands on him'.[13] Nobody likes to be told they are living a lie. It should come as no surprise that Platonism became very popular with an early Christianity trying to establish its respectability in a world dominated by Greek culture. Bertrand Russell goes so far as to claim that 'The theology of St Paul and of the Fathers was largely derived from [Plato] directly or indirectly, and can hardly be understood if Plato is ignored'.[14] The idea of a real world beyond this world of appearances and of a misunderstood and ultimately doomed saviour figure who enters the world of shadows and illusion to lead us into the light has a powerful messianic resonance. Indeed the notion of our being trapped in a shared hallucination from which we need to be woken up by an heroic messiah is one that has been fairly recently revisited in *The Matrix* trilogy of films which present us with Plato's analogy of the cave in all but name.[15]

Clarity and distinctiveness

Rene Descartes (1596–1650), often referred to as the father of modern philosophy, was in his own context as anxious as Plato concerning the potential impact of scepticism. As the Renaissance encouraged both independent thinking and experimentation the traditional authorities upon which western culture had been based for centuries – principally the Greek classics and the Christian scriptures – began to be viewed with suspicion. If we can no longer rely upon authorised religion and metaphysics to provide us with a basis for truth then where do we turn if we are to avoid the chaos of relativism? Descartes famously sought to address this problem by establishing an unquestionable foundation for certainty not dependent upon any external authority. His epistemology, that is to say his theory of knowledge, rests upon the famous statement 'cogito ergo sum' – I think, therefore I am. Descartes reasoned that the one thing that each individual can be certain of with absolute clarity is that they are thinking, irrespective of what they may be thinking of. If I am aware of my own consciousness then it follows that there exists an 'I' having this experience. Even if one is being deceived by God or some other higher power, one's existence cannot be questioned:

> There is therefore no doubt that I exist, if he deceives me; and let him deceive me as much as he likes, he can never cause me to be nothing, so long as I think I am something. So that, after having thought carefully about it, and having scrupulously examined everything, one must then, in conclusion, take as assured that the proposition: I am, I exist, is necessarily true, every time I express it or conceive of it in my mind.[16]

In other words, you may very well be in the Matrix but at least there is a 'you' to be in it. Descartes argued that the *cogito* coupled with a belief in a benevolent God – something that he also tried to demonstrate was self-evident and indubitable – was enough to provide us with a foundation for certainty in our quest for truth thus saving us from the dangers of scepticism and anarchy.

So Descartes' response to the potential for anarchy and epistemological relativism attendant upon the increasing loss of confidence in traditional authorities was to seek a new foundation for absolute truth. This he found in the notion of 'the cogito', the undeniable awareness that I have of my own existence from one thinking moment to the next. Descartes sought to govern his epistemological explorations by the strict observation of four laws, the first and foremost being:

> 'never to accept anything as true that I did not know to be evidently so: that is to say, carefully to avoid precipitancy and prejudice, and to include in my judgments nothing more than what presented itself so clearly and so distinctly to my mind that I might have no occasion to place it in doubt.'[17]

Descartes argues that it is the undeniable clarity and distinctness of the truth 'I think therefore I am' which makes it convincing. It was the establishing of clarity and distinctiveness as the twin criteria for ascertaining truth which was to become programmatic for Enlightenment epistemology and the bane of the imagination. Something is clear if it is so vivid and powerful that it cannot be avoided and something is distinct if it cannot be confused with anything else. Thus knowledge became inextricably intertwined with the notion of precision.

In the wake of the Cartesian epistemology there followed a succession of philosophers who sought to develop and refine our understanding of what truth is and how we apprehend it. John Locke, denied the existence of innate ideas, ideas we are born with, and related all knowledge to sense data – we are *blank slates* to be written on by our sense experiences. David Hume, argued for epistemic scepticism in general and criticised religious experience, such as miracles, in particular. Immanuel Kant, went on to deny the very possibility of any metaphysical knowledge, that is knowledge that goes beyond the sensory.

It could be argued that what Plato is to classical philosophy Immanuel Kant (1724–1804) is to modern philosophy. Whatever one may think of Kant it is impossible to deny his central role in the development of modern western philosophy and theology. Kant's concern with scepticism was catalysed by his encounter with the work of the Scottish philosopher David Hume. At a moment in history when natural science was in the ascendant and confidence in the experimental method pioneered by Francis Bacon was riding high, Hume threw a sceptical spanner in the works by arguing that the so-called laws of nature such as cause and effect were based on nothing more than habit and custom. According to Hume the only reason that we identify something as a law of nature is because it has, so far, always behaved in a certain way, however, it does not logically follow that it always will. So, an object thrown out of a ten-storey building will fall to earth at a certain speed under the force of gravity. However, argues Hume, the only way one can know for certain that the same thing will happen again would be to repeat the action. Any statement that it must always happen is nothing more than a prediction and not an empirical certainty.

Kant was concerned that Hume's thinking would open the way to a new scepticism that threatened to undo the fragile new absolutes that human reason and natural science had to offer in place of traditional religious and metaphysical authorities. In his most famous work *The Critique of Pure Reason* he argues that what we called the absolute laws of nature, for example, cause and effect and even space and time, are not to be found in the external world but are actually categories of thought, part of our reasoning tool kit. In essence the world appears ordered because we as rational beings order it. Our reason sorts through the data gathered by our senses and puts it together in meaningful patterns like some huge jigsaw puzzle. It follows that anything not open to our senses cannot be dealt with in this way and thus is not, according to Kant, real knowledge – clearly a significant threat to religious epistemology. Of course, while Kant saw this as a way of avoiding scepticism and establishing order he was never able to demonstrate why each individual's reason should operate in the same way, nor indeed could he according to the lights of his own critical philosophy as another's human reason is not open to investigation via our senses.

So through the Enlightenment, knowledge was actually being redefined, vast areas of human data were being rejected as real knowledge as rigid criteria were laid down for establishing what constituted knowledge and what did not. At the heart of it all sat the Cartesian knowing subject occupying a position of absolute epistemic privilege, a position, incidentally, recently vacated by God.

This was a time when natural science and its hero Newton were in ascendance, everyone wanted to be the Newton of their own discipline, bringing order out of chaos. The universe was now being understood as a self-perpetuating mechanism, perhaps started by God, which could be understood completely if watched carefully. It was a law abiding mechanism which ran consistently according to laws such as the law of gravitation. To understand this world and our place in it did not require imaginative speculation or storytelling, it required precise observation, measurement and recording.

Images and imagination fast came to be seen as, at best, second rate ways of accessing the world and, at worst, actually misleading. An image, became not 'a' way of portraying reality but a pale copy of something more real – something more accurately and clearly described via natural science. The German idealist philosopher Hegel made a similar point when he argued that religion – and he had Christianity in mind here – was essentially a less sophisticated way of portraying the abstract truths of philosophy. Religion used images such as Father, Son and Holy Spirit to convey to the less educated and less able a sense of the dialectic, the logical foundation of the universe by which the universal spirit progressively comes to an awareness of itself. Such philosophical ideas may only be grasped in their true form by very few, however the less precise images of religion may be appreciated by many more.

Movements such as Logical Positivism, developed during the 1920s and championed by British philosophers such as A.J.Ayer, Bertrand Russell and the early Ludwig Wittgenstein, took this perspective as far as it would go arguing that unless a word corresponded to an actual something in the world then it was meaningless. Language was thus understood as a precise labelling tool and it followed that if there was nothing to stick a particular label on to then that label was meaningless. Russell's famous example of this was the sentence 'The present king of France is bald'. This is a sentence which sounds like it means something as all the words are understandable and the grammar is correct. However, according to Russell this is a meaningless statement as there is no King of France, there is nothing in the world upon which we can hang the label 'the king of France' and hence it is a vacuous term. Russell argues that religious state-ments are meaningless for precisely the same reason. While the statement 'God is love' might sound like it has meaning we cannot actually attach the label 'God' to anything in the world. Interestingly enough, as Wittgenstein would later realise, it is equally problematic to find something in the world that the label 'love' may be attached to. Nevertheless, and perhaps somewhat surprisingly, it was Russell who also observed:

> Imagination is the goad that forces human beings into rest-less exertion after their primary needs have been satisfied … While animals are content with existence and reproduction, men desire also to expand, and their desires in this respect are limited only by what imagination suggests as possible.[18]

In his famous early work the *Tractatus Logico-Philosophicus*, first published in English in 1922, Wittgenstein makes this same point in his own way by opening with the statement 'The world is everything that is the case' and closing 'What we cannot speak about we must pass over in silence'.[19] Such a view saw the imaginative use of language as frivolous and ultimately pointless if perhaps entertaining. Wittgenstein goes further when he makes the claim: 'If a question can be put at all, then it can also be answered'.

So we see that many of the key points in the history of western philosophy are characterised by the quest for absolutes, for certainty and for an unambiguous perception of the world, and that reason has been most frequently identified as the source or medium of such certainty and unambiguous perception. It is not surprising then that the human capacity for the imaginative has often been viewed with suspicion. Imagination is one of those human capacities, such as emotion and intuition, that while formally receiving rather a bad press in a technologically orientated culture, is nevertheless acknowledged to play an important role in our day-to-day lives. Consider for a moment the dismissive ways in which imagination and related terms such as speculation, story and myth are often dealt with in our culture:

'You just imagined it'
'She has an over-active imagination'
'That's just an image, not the real thing'
'That is purely speculative'
'That isn't real, it's just a story'
'That isn't really true, it's just a myth'

The products of the imagination are considered, for various reasons which we shall consider shortly, somehow less 'real', less 'true' and thus less 'relevant'. On the other hand, in certain contexts we reward people for their imagination:

'That was a very imaginative solution to the problem'
'That was very intuitive of you'
'That was a powerful story'
'That is a potent or moving image'

And despite the history of growing suspicion outlined above, philosophers have also sought to emphasise the power of our capacity for imagination. A range of influential thinkers have made the point that there is more to the world than meets the eye, and that reason and logic are not the only ways to paint an authentic and significant picture of that world. The rehabilitation of the importance of the imagination, championed in a variety of ways by both the romantic and postmodern movements, will serve to support our choice of imaginative sources and the stimulus for our exploration of the heroic and the villainous.

Jacques Derrida – quoting Immanuel Kant in the *Critique of Judgement* – has this to say:

Imagination is the freedom that reveals itself only in its works. These works do not exist within nature, but neither do they inhabit a world other than ours. ' The imagination ... is a powerful agent for creating, as it were, a second nature out of the material supplied to it by actual nature'. This is why intelligence is not necessarily the essential faculty of the critic when he sets out to encounter imagination and beauty; 'in what we call beautiful, intelligence is at the service of the imagination ...' [20]

The return of imagination

During and since the Enlightenment there have been two movements that have sought to revive the significance of imagination within western culture.

1. Romanticism
2. Postmodernism

Both of these – in their own unique ways – have sought to argue for the importance of imagination as a means of exploring ourselves and our world, particularly as these explorations reach the borders of sense experience and enter the realms of emotion, the mysterious and the religious.

While Enlightenment thinkers and artists favoured a uniform understanding of humankind that did not vary substantially across time or geography, the Romantics generally encouraged individual expression and difference.

Jean-Jacques Rousseau, arguably the first of the Romantics and certainly one of the principal architects of the movement, both championed a view of music which saw it as expressive of our inner nature, our emotional landscape if you will, and also wrote what is widely regarded as the prototypical romantic novel *La nouvelle Heloise* in 1761. Maurice Cranston writes of this work:

> The message of the novel was seen as a liberating one; that the imagination need no longer be the slave of reason, that feelings should not be suppressed, denied in the name of decorum; that if only one could strip away the falseness and pretence by which modern society was dominated, there was goodness to be discovered in the human heart.[21]

This message and indeed the general format of the story can be seen in other romantic works such as Goethe's *Die Leiden des jungen Werther* and, of course, Emily Bronte's *Wuthering Heights*.

Romanticism soon came to be regarded as an alternative spirituality of sorts, a way of opposing the Enlightenment's prioritising of reason and sense data while avoiding falling back into what were seen as outmoded religious habits and customs. God was replace with nature and Jesus was recast in the form of the doomed anti-hero so beloved of romantic writers. The imagination was understood by the majority, but interestingly not all,[22] of the romantics as the primary route to understanding. Diderot, a great friend of Rousseau, maintained that science ought properly to be founded upon imagination and conjecture rather than upon empirical observation. It is, according to Diderot, in the examination of the unusual and the original that we gain insight into the true nature of the world rather than in the cataloguing of mechanical processes in the manner of the Newtonian scientist.

For example, in *Milton: a Poem* published around 1811, William Blake, expressed his mission as:

> To bathe in the Waters of Life, to wash off the Not Human
> I come in Self-Annihilation and the grandeur of Inspiration
> To cast off Rational Demonstration by Faith in the Saviour
> To cast off the rotten rags of Memory by Inspiration
> To cast off Bacon, Locke and Newton from Albion's covering
> To take off his filthy garments and clothe him in
>   imagination.[23]

Compare this to a similar sentiment expressed by Wordsworth in 'The Tables Turned' (1798) when he wrote:

> Sweet is the lore which nature brings;
> Our meddling intellect
> Misshapes the beauteous forms of things:–
> We murder to dissect.
>
> Enough of science and of art;
> Close up those barren leaves;
> Come forth, and bring with you a heart
> That watches and receives.[24]

For the romantic life was far too complex and too wondrous to analyse without remainder, to reduce to Cartesian clarity and distinctiveness. Indeed, it seems to me that this is the very hallmark of the hero, to engage with life in all its messy multi-facetedness, to recognise that the world cannot be made right simply by following a formula or a procedure.

That nebulous intellectual and cultural movement known as Postmodernism further endorses the idea that human existence is not susceptible to precise definition. Many postmoderns go so far as to argue that all we ever have are image and imagination, that there is no one truth, no absolute reality, that these images clearly and distinctly correspond to.[25] While it could be argued that Postmodernism's rejection of absolute value only serves to undermine the notion of the hero – how can one fight for truth and justice when these are regarded as empty terms? Its recognition of the limits of human reason and its identification of the world as infinitely complex, thus defying reduction to a single explanatory story, or grand narrative, provides us with an insight into the context of the truly heroic.

The hero is the one who accepts, however unpalatable this might be, that human existence defies our best attempts at reduction and categorisation. In this sense, as I hope we shall discover throughout this book, part of being a hero has to do with *being in the world* in a certain way. A way which acknowledges the glorious complexity of human existence while at the same time recognising its dark obverse – the potential for violence and chaos. It is in this mode of existence in the world that the hero may be seen as taking on a divine quality in that God, certainly within the Christian tradition, is understood as creating and relating to a humanity endowed with freedom. It is this freedom that gives rise to both our uniqueness and capacity for self-giving and creative choice while at the same time permitting us to adopt a self-serving, destructive and dysfunctional path. It is the unenviable fate of the hero to stand between these two possibilities, to stand at the border of freedom and chaos.

2

The Outsider:
Heroes and Otherness

One of the characteristic marks of the hero is what we might call their transcendental status. That is to say the hero, while in a very real sense being part of the world and caught up in the human condition, is at the same time understood as standing outside of the world we know. Indeed, the very power and capabilities of the hero are dependent upon their capacity to transcend the mundane world and thus to bring into it salvific powers unavailable to ordinary humanity. Campbell puts it like this:

> The standard path of the mythological adventure of the hero is a magnification of the formula represented in the rites of passage: separation – initiation – return: ... A hero ventures forth from the world of common day into a region of super-natural wonder: fabulous forces are there encountered and a decisive victory is won: the hero comes back from the mysterious adventure with the power to bestow boons on his fellow man.[1]

The beyond, or some aspect of otherness, as a necessary ingredient for the heroic comes in many different forms but it seems to me that its purpose is always the same. As Campbell points out the hero in some way derives both the power to aid the rest of humanity and the desire to do so from a position of otherness and distance. As Stan Lee wrote in the first ever Spiderman comic story 'with great power comes great responsibility' and this would certainly seem to be a major motif within the heroic character, as we shall see.

The word transcendence derives from the Latin *transcendo* meaning 'to go beyond'. The term has generally come to be used to describe anything that exceeds the human ability to access in any conventional way.[2] God is frequently defined as transcendent in that the divine being exists in a mode that is both outside our comprehension and which is furthermore alien to our own existence. In this sense God is often understood as both epistemologically and ontologically transcendent. This view, while not universally held even within the Christian tradition,[3] is a function of the view that God created the cosmos as an entity completely separate from God's own being. Of course one of the central problems that has plagued religions with an adherence to a transcendent divinity is, how does one reconcile the necessary otherness of God with the equally important belief that God is somehow sympathetic to the human condition and involved in human affairs? This is the paradox of transcendence and immanence, how God can be beyond and other while at the same time present and intimate. The Christian theologian Dietrich Bonhoeffer captures something of the essence of this paradox when he writes:

> God's 'beyond' is not the beyond of our cognitive faculties. The transcendence of epistemological theory has nothing to do with the transcendence of God. God is beyond in the midst of our life.[4]

Of course, the problem of how to overcome otherness is by no means unique to a transcendent God. In a very real sense it is a problem that every human being has to wrestle with from the moment they are born. The fact that we are other than the cosmos and everything we encounter in it is a constant source of both anxiety and wonder for us. We spend much of our life struggling for ways in which to codify our sense of self, or inner life, our sense of unique identity in an attempt to transmit it to others. We are, undoubtedly in the first instance at least, an alienated species. We are forever looking for ways in which to 'put ourselves out there' to 'leave a mark' on the world and the people we meet. The fact that nobody truly understands us is a source of anxiety that begins to hit us in our early teens and which, while we learnt to cope with it, never really goes away. Yet it is this very uniqueness, the fact that we are other than everything else in the entire cosmos, which gives us our greatest power – to contribute something that nobody else can, to 'be' in the world in a way that nobody else can.

This situation, it seems to me, is written large in both the figure of the hero and the villain. The transcendent/immanent paradox, the distinction between the self and the other, is one which typifies the heroic figure in a variety of forms and ironically in most cases it is precisely the transcendentally resourced power of the hero which marks them out as tragic and lonely figures.

One girl in all the world

One of the most significant and popular heroic figures of the late twentieth early twenty-first century has been Buffy Summers from the *Buffy The Vampire Slayer* TV series. With this character many of the traditional heroic – and villainous – motifs have been both revisited and recast.

The *Buffy* series clearly operates at a number of levels but it is at its metaphorical level that we gain the greatest insight into both the nature of the hero but also into the heroic necessities of everyday life.

On the face of it Buffy Summers is a typical, almost caricatured, angst ridden, fashion conscious teenage girl. She is concerned with shopping, being popular and dating boys. However, there are two special things about her life that define her as something other than just a normal girl. First of all, her school, Sunnydale High, is situated over a Hellmouth, a literal gateway to the underworld with all the attendant demonic activity you would expect to come pouring out of it. Secondly, and most importantly, Buffy is The Slayer, the chosen one, as the opening narration from the first episode puts it: 'In every generation, there is a chosen one. She alone will stand against the vampires, the demons, and the forces of darkness. She is the slayer.'

The operative words here for the moment are 'chosen one' and 'alone', for while Buffy surrounds herself with good friends who support her in her fight against evil there is a very strong motif pursued throughout the series that she is essentially and finally alone. This theme comes to a powerful conclusion in the last series where Buffy frequently makes this point in connection with her sole responsibility for the deaths of those around her, but also in the way that the tradition of the solitary Slayer is dismantled by her. We shall return to this point later.

What actually makes Buffy such a classic solitary heroic figure is an interesting issue not least because the nature of this heroic isolation, often while still in the presence of her closest friends, is, I would suggest, completely familiar to us all. While it is true that Buffy possesses super powers beyond those of ordinary human beings – mega strength, enhanced reflexes and agility – it is not these that make her heroic, many less heroic figures possess similar abilities within the series. What marks Buffy out is her sense of moral responsibility coupled with clear recognition of the ethical demands made on the self by the other.

This sense of ethical duty, what we 'ought' to do in any given situation rather than what we would like to do finds its clearest and most enduring expression in the work of the eighteenth century philosopher Emmanuel Kant.

It is the unconditioned character of the human will free from the determination of the sensible world that stands as the source of all true ethical activity for Kant. In other words, freedom, or the autonomy of the will, the uncoerced ability to determine what one *ought* to do is to be regarded as, what Kant calls, a necessary *postulate of practical reason*, and represents the true form of human morality.

The content of human morality is often determined by consideration of consequences such as the greater good or self-satisfaction, or the betterment of the species. This, argues Kant, is an insufficient basis for universal moral law. To perform our duty, to act as we ought for the sake of the moral law, and not simply for some desired end as a consequence of moral activity, demands both that the moral law itself be unconditioned, and that we, as rational beings, be free from all determination as regards our compliance with it. 'Ought', argues Kant, implies 'can'. What the moral law demands of us we must be free to perform. It is in the light of this freedom, manifesting itself in the autonomy of the will that we may regard ourselves as 'independent of determination by causes in the sensible world'[5] bound only by the laws of reason. Being conditioned by the empirical world or laws of nature Kant refers to as heteronomy, while determination solely by the rational will be called autonomy. It is only the autonomous will, free to choose, that can act ethically.

It is the very formality of what Kant calls the 'principle of volition' or 'the principle of the will' which establishes the moral worth of rational, ethical behaviour. All material motives are to be abandoned in the quest for unconditioned moral worth:

> Where then can this worth be found if we are not to find it in the will's relation to the effect hoped for from the action? It can be found nowhere but in the principle of the will, irrespective of the ends which can be brought about by such an action; for between its a priori principle, which is formal, and its a posteriori motive, which is material, the will stands, so to speak, at a parting of the ways; and since it must be determined by some principle, it will have to be determined by the formal principle of volition when an action is done from duty, where, as we have seen, every material principle is taken away from it.[6]

By virtue of the autonomy of the will every individual, as an unconditioned rational being, must consider him/herself to be the maker of universal law. This making of universal law in so far as it does not depend upon any cause other than the rational will establishes all rational beings as ends in themselves. The notion of rational beings as ends in themselves rather than as means to an end is absolutely central for Kant's understanding of personhood.

All rational beings, claims Kant, must be regarded as ends in themselves and never as means. It is *things* and not *people* that are conditioned and rigidly dependent upon nature and its laws and thus, while things are ultimately of relative value, people are of absolute value.

> Persons, therefore, are not merely subjective ends whose existence as an object of our actions has a value for us: they are objective ends – that is, things whose existence is in itself an end ... [7]

It is this understanding of rational beings as *ends* rather than *means* that forms the foundation of what Kant refers to as the 'Kingdom of ends'. A rational being is a member of this Kingdom when they subject themselves to the very laws they seek to establish. This idea finds its most celebrated expression in the Kantian maxim:

> Act in such a way that you always treat humanity, whether in your own person or in the person of any other, never simply as a means, but always at the same time as an end. [8]

Thus for Kant the true rational person, must acknowledge all others both as ends, as autonomous law-makers – this then is the very foundation of Kantian ethics. The noted Kant commentator E. Cassirer expresses it this way:

> all rational beings stand under the law so that in constituting their personhood, they are in relation with the moral individuality of all others, and so that they also demand the fundamental worth which they thus grant themselves from every other subject and acknowledge it in all other subjects.[9]

This view of the dignity and worth of the other in the face of all other considerations of taste and motivation is of primary significance for Buffy as the Slayer, the chosen one. People cannot and must not be used as means, not even if it is apparently for the greater good.

The Season Five finale 'The Gift' demonstrates this defining dimension to Buffy's heroic character in two powerfully poignant ways. Firstly, in her refusal to kill Ben, an innocent human being who nevertheless, and against his wishes, provides the means for the malevolent deity Glory to manifest herself in the world (by essentially sharing the same body) and bring about its destruction. Buffy manages to subdue Glory at which point Ben regains control of the shared body and Buffy walks away. While Ben lies on the ground suffering from the physical damage sustained by the body he shares with Glory during her fight with Buffy, Rupert Giles – Buffy's mentor and ersatz father figure – approaches:

> GILES: Can you move?
>
> BEN: *(in pain)* Need a minute. She could have killed me.
>
> GILES: No, she couldn't, never, and sooner or later Glory will re-emerge and make Buffy pay for that mercy and the world with her. Buffy even knows that and still she couldn't take a human life. She's a hero you see, she's not like us.

With that, Giles covers the injured Ben's face with his hand and suffocates him.

Throughout the series the character of Buffy sacrifices happiness, success, love and even life (twice!) in her heroic battle with the forces of evil. Everything she is is fundamentally orientated towards the other. From her position as the chosen one, the *one girl in all the world* who can protect us from the dark, she overcomes her loneliness, the transcendental gulf between her and the world, by offering herself up to that world. It is this that distinguishes the hero from the villain. In the face of the isolation that difference can generate the hero gives him or her self over to the world, and in so doing re-enters the world. The villain, on the other hand, deepens the gulf between self and other and sees dominance of the other as the only mode of engagement between themselves and the rest of the world. Buffy, for example, longs to be an ordinary girl, part of the world, while for the most part her villainous counterparts wish to be as gods, distant from the world, dominating and controlling it from afar.

The second profoundly heroic moment in the Season Five finale is where Buffy sacrifices her life both for her sister in particular and for the world in general. While Glory herself was being defeated by Buffy, her minions succeed in opening up a portal to a hell dimension that would eventually spill out destroying all worlds in its wake. The only way to seal the portal is by a blood sacrifice from Buffy's sister or someone related to her. Buffy hurls herself into the rift closing it and ending her life. As she falls we hear her last words to her sister:

> BUFFY: Dawn, listen to me. Listen. I love you. I will *always* love you. But this is the work that I have to do. Tell Giles … tell Giles I figured it out. And, and I'm okay. And give my love to my friends. You have to take care of them now. You have to take care of each other. You have to be strong. Dawn, the hardest thing in this world … is to live in it. Be brave. Live. For me.

In this Buffy expresses the very nature of the heroic as suggested in our opening chapter. It is being in the world in a particular way that truly establishes an heroic mode of existence. How we choose to live in a world which assails us constantly with choices and options and ill-defined complexities is what marks out each moment of our lives as heroic or otherwise. It is telling that in the final scene in this *Buffy* episode we see Buffy's grave stone which reads:

Buffy Anne Summers
1981–2001
Devoted Sister
Beloved Friend
She Saved the World
A Lot

The reference to her adventurous, world saving heroics is, I believe, deliberately understated as this is not, in the final analysis, what made her a hero.

Self-giving, to the point of self abandonment and the risk of destruction, becomes in the *Buffy* series, not only the heroic ideal but simply *the way to be in the world*. All of Buffy's friends and even one of her most bitter enemies, the vampire Spike, learn this and achieve a level of personal redemption through it. Willow as she comes to terms with her unique power and its capacity to consume her finally chooses to risk this possible fate for the sake of others. Xander, who has his most obvious heroic moment when he confronts a Willow driven mad with power with nothing but his love for her, is nonetheless at his most heroic when he explains that his true power is to be out of the spotlight where he can better see and hear his friends' needs. Anya, who spent much of her long life as a vengeance demon punishing men in a variety of gruesome ways ends her life fighting to protect one. Spike of course is a classic example of heroic redemption. Starting out his adult life in the eighteenth century as a foppish and rather ineffectual romantic, he becomes a vampire and his undead existence is one of cruelty and brutality that is remarkable even by vampire standards. His frequent encounters with Buffy lead him, eventually, through a quest for his immortal soul which threatens to topple him over into permanent insanity. The scenes in the final series where Spike is half mad with remorse are among some of the most poignant in the entire *Buffy* saga. The scene from the final season episode 'Beneath You' where Buffy confronts Spike in a church is particularly memorable:

BUFFY: No more mind games Spike

SPIKE: No more mind games. No more mind.

BUFFY: Tell me what happened.

SPIKE: I tried to find it of course.

BUFFY: Find what?

SPIKE: The spark, the missing … the piece that fit … that would make me fit … because you didn't want … Angel, he should have warned me … its here, in me, all the time, the spark. I wanted to give you what you deserve and I got it. They put the spark in me and now all it does is burn.

BUFFY: Your soul.

SPIKE: Bit worse for lack of use.

BUFFY: You got your soul back, how?

SPIKE: It's what you wanted, right? (eyes to heaven) it's what You wanted, right? And now, everybody's in here (grasping at his head) talking, everything I did, everyone I … everybody telling me to go, go to hell … And she will look on him with forgiveness and everyone will forgive and love and will be loved. (*embraces a cross and is seared by it*) So everything is okay, right? Can we rest now? Buffy? Can we rest?

Spike's desire for Buffy – ultimately resulting in his attempted rape of her – forces him to realise the distinction between desire, and the attendant need to control through possession and violence, and love. It is this newly awakened awareness that constitutes the true return of Spike's soul rather than the mythical tests we see him endure in a previous episode. Thus the villainous Spike who tried to take Buffy by force at the end of Season Six is replaced by the heroic Spike who is content simply to hold her while she rests and describes this one incident as 'the best night of his life'.

As with Buffy's previous lover Angel, another vicious vampire who has his soul returned as a punishment, the possession of a soul appears to go hand in hand with a sense of responsibility and conscience. Both Angel and Spike, once ensouled, find the memories of the evil they have inflicted almost impossible to bear. Indeed, it is this sense of remorse that can be seen to fuel their various heroic activities. This is most powerfully portrayed in the final episode of the *Buffy* saga when it is the light of Spike's soul that both destroys the Hellmouth while at the same time consuming Spike himself.

The *Buffy* series is as much to do with living a normal life in a world that is always other and often antagonistic to us as it is to do with battling demonic forces. Much of the early series can be read as a metaphor for coping with adolescence – dealing with the day-to-day horrors of school life such as making friends, establishing an identity, coping with a variety of emotions and handling success and failure. One of the most significant things Buffy ever does, in my view, is befriend the school 'losers' Willow and Xander thus alienating herself from the 'in crowd' of beautiful people typified by Cordelia Chase. To deliberately court unpopularity on your first day at a new school is a truly heroic act!

* * *

'With great power there must also come ... great responsibility!' – *Amazing Fantasy 15*, 1962 (The first appearance of Spiderman)

If there were a single sentence that summed up the *raison d'etre* of the comic book super hero, and the essential nature of their distinction from the world – then the above quote from Stan Lee – the original writer of the Spiderman stories – would be a serious candidate. Compare this with the definition of the hero given by Joseph Campbell:

> The hero is the man of self-achieved submission. But submission to what? That precisely is the riddle that today we have to ask ourselves and that it is everywhere the primary virtue and historic deed of the hero to have solved.[10]

Campbell, arguing along Jungian lines, suggests that the mythic hero can be seen as representing a single ideal, a monomyth, which has manifested itself through the world's literature and religions for thousands of years[11] – he includes figures such as Moses, Gautama Buddha and Jesus here – and he laments the lack of such myths today.

While there may be some truth in this – especially in view of the decline in the value placed upon the imagination since the Enlightenment (cf. Chapter One) – this is, I believe, an overstatement. J. Shelton and R. Jewett in their book *The Myth of the American Superhero* make a similar point when they comment on Campbell's belief in the absence of modern myths.

> We disagree. The widespread current enthusiasm for materials such as *The Matrix*, *Rambo*, *Touched by an Angel*, and the *Star Trek*, *Star Wars*, and left behind franchises indicate that Americans have not moved beyond mythical consciousness.[12]

The comic book superhero is, to my mind, one of the most mythologically charged creative products of the twentieth and twenty-first centuries. Nowhere else do we find such a rich collection of archetypal heroic and villainous characters endlessly renewed and recast for each generation reflecting and manifesting contemporary culture's highest values and greatest fears.

Since the early part of the twentieth century American comic books have provided us with a staggering array of super powered individuals whose lives and abilities have been dedicated to the war against evil and villainy wherever it may be found and however it my be construed. Developing out of the newspaper adventure strips of the 1920s featuring extraordinary but none the less human heroes such as Buck Rodgers and Tarzan, the costumed *super* hero represented a new mythology which tapped into a war-weary cultures desire for protection, unassailable power and unambiguous moral superiority – something, I believe, we still see reflected in the USA's attitude to it's military today.

It was during the early 1930s that the first super hero appeared in the form of the template for many, if not all, subsequent paranormal costumed heroes – Superman. While there had been heroes, even costumed heroes, previous to the formal 1938 début of the 'Man of Steel', in *Action Comics Number 1*, Superman struck a mythic chord which has become part of American if not international culture ever since. The story of the child sent by his father and mother from a doomed world to Earth, there to be adopted by human parents and later to discover his possession of superhuman powers that he chooses to use for the betterment of mankind is all but messianic in its impact. The notion of a transcendent saviour with powers beyond our own exercising benevolent impartiality is a potent one and one that Superman, up to a point, embodies.

Superman, or Kal-El as we discover his real name to be, as an iconic hero fighting for 'truth, justice and the American way' is other than the world he fights for in the most complete way possible. As an alien refugee from the doomed planet of Krypton Kal-El adopts Earth and its people as his own. While many costumed heroes took on alternate heroic identities, assuming *alter egos* so as to better combat evil and villainy behind often quite literal masks of anonymity, Kal-El's *alter ego* was in fact his human persona, that of Clark Kent. As Clark Kent, Kal-El hides his Superman persona both out of fear of his enemies targeting his vulnerable human friends as a way of getting at him but also to engage with the world as an ordinary human being.

In Quentin Tarantino's film *Kill Bill Vol. 2* the eponymous Bill makes this exact same point:

> Superman stands alone. Superman did not become Superman. Superman was born Superman. When Superman wakes up in the morning, he is Superman. His *alter ego* is Clark Kent. His outfit with the big red S is the blanket he was wrapped in as a baby when the Kents found him. Those are his clothes. What Kent wears, the glasses, the business suit, that's the costume Superman wears to blend in with us. Clark Kent is how Superman views us. Clark Kent is Superman's critique on the whole human race.[13]

In a very real sense while Superman is the adventurer it could be argued that it is Clark Kent who is truly heroic. It is Kent who has to sensitively navigate his way through a world in which he could be a god. Kal-El plays his Clark Kent persona as a weak and often bumbling individual so as to draw attention away from any possible identification with Superman. Due to his need to take on his Superman identity in times of crisis, Clark Kent is generally seen as running away from danger and is often considered cowardly for this reason. For a great deal of his career Kal-El had to cope with the love of his life – Lois Lane – being madly in love with Superman while being romantically completely indifferent to Clark Kent. Incidentally, this is a much used theme within the comic super hero tradition where one of the hero's two *alter egos* is the object of love and affection while the other is either ignored or even actively despised. We see this, for example, in the relationship between Don Blake (good hearted but weak and physically handicapped doctor), his later ego Thor (the Norse god of thunder) and Jane Foster, Blake's nurse. In some of the earliest Thor stories we find Jane day dreaming about ironing Thor's cape and trimming his hair while bemoaning the fact that Don Blake, who is deeply in love with her but says nothing, appears cowardly and weak.[14] The character of Spiderman was idolised by Flash Thompson – the school 'jock' – while his bookish *alter ego* Peter Parker was mercilessly bullied by him. Later on it was Spiderman who was often vilified in the press and feared by those who were actually closest to Peter – his doting Aunt May for example.[15] In many respects the ingredients that made Spiderman such a popular figure particularly during the 1960s and 1970s – his apparently weak *alter ego*, his alienation from the 'in crowd', his sense of responsibility to those around him and the fact that his super powers didn't actually help him to cope with growing up, are precisely the elements that made the Buffy series so popular in the late 1990s and early 2000s.

Once again, we seem to encounter the heroic not so much in the exercise of power and paranormal ability, but in terms of how the world is engaged with and how otherness is overcome. There are many instances when the above mentioned heroes, for example, are tempted to try and use their unique abilities to serve themselves, to make life easier, as a short cut to personal satisfaction. While this is the primary *modus operandi* of the villain, the hero invariably resists this temptation, as messianic figures always do when tested, and chooses instead to suffer the pain of the world alongside ordinary humanity – we see this theme particularly emphasised in Tolkien's *The Lord of the Rings* where it is the power of Sauron's ring that poses the temptation, more on this later. Take for example a scene from *The Amazing Spiderman Number 4* published in 1963 when the character was still in its infancy. Spiderman having defeated a super powered villain in full view of his adoring school peers returns to his identity as Peter Parker:

GIRL: Well, well, look who's here! 'Mr Book Worm of 1963!'

FLASH: Now that the fighting's over, you finally came out of hiding, eh?

PETER: You brainless loud-mouth! You've insulted me for the last time! I'm gonna wipe that stupid leer off your face right now!

FLASH: Well, well! So the worm finally turned, eh? I've been waiting for this!

PETER *(thinking)*: Wait! What am I doing?? I can't lose my temper like this! With the strength of Spider-Man, if I get into a fight with a normal guy I could pulverize him!

PETER: Aww, forget it! You're not even worth the trouble! I've got more important things to do!

FLASH: Sure, things like chickening out of fights, and hiding whenever there's trouble! Things like that can keep a fella real busy can't they, Petey boy?[16]

The truly heroic mode of engagement with the world, with the other, is one in which the other always presents one with an ethical responsibility irrespective of the ways in which that other might confront us. The refusal to dominate as the primary mode of relating to the world is a characteristic trait of the hero and this is often in the face of aggression and abuse. Compare the attitude and behaviour of Peter Parker in the above quote with that of the super villain Kid Marvelman. In spite of his rather disarming name, the character of Kid Marvelman is a chilling example of the villain's total disregard for the other in exercising his or her power to dominate.

Marvelman (later renamed Miracleman for copyright reasons) and his young sidekick Kid Marvelman were originally stereo-typical 1950s superman copies however they were reinvented in the 1980s by Alan Moore who gave the series a much darker contemporary edge. At the end of the original series Marvelman and Kid Marvelman had both, apparently, been destroyed in an atomic blast however, in the 1980s series, we discover that they had in fact both survived: Marvelman in a state of severe amnesia (such that he had forgotten that he had the ability to transform himself into a super powered being), and Kid Marvelman having chosen to remain in his super powered form all the time rather than return to his human *alter ego*, that of Johnny Bates. Marvelman regains his memory after twenty years and is reunited with his now highly successful former partner but begins to sense that something is not right:

MARVELMAN: John, I listened to your story just now … rags to riches, redemption through honest toil. It's a great story. I really wanted to believe it, John. But then halfway through I got this funny idea into my head. I thought 'What if he's lying?' I tried to get rid of it. I tried. But I couldn't. I thought 'What if he survived that blast … and was still Kid Marvelman?' I tried to imagine what it would feel like … to be the most powerful creature on the face of the planet … and to be answerable to no-one. You could do anything, John, you'd never need to turn back to dull, weak, human Johnny Bates ever again. Oh sure, you could take his name, his identity ... but you could stay as Kid Marvelman forever. You could have it all ... money, prestige, fame ... you could sever all your links with humanity. You could become remorseless, unstoppable ... and totally corrupt. Is that it, John? Is that what happened? You're still Kid Marvelman aren't you? I can tell by your voice, by the way you stand ... you're not human, John. I can feel it.[17]

It is hardly surprising that the project that gave the Marvelman team their powers was called 'Project Zarathustra' - a reference to Nietzsche's famous work in which he introduced the notion of the Superman. For Nietzsche, the Superman was not a being in possession of paranormal powers but one who transcended all values and conventions:

I teach you the Superman. Man is something that is to be surpassed... What is the greatest thing ye can experience? It is the hour of great contempt. The hour in which even your happiness becomes loathsome unto you, and so also your reason and virtue... The hour when ye say: 'What good is my virtue! As yet it hath not made me passionate. How weary I am of my good and my bad! It is all poverty and pollution and wretched self-complacency!

The Hour when ye say: 'What good is my justice! I do not see that I am fervour and fuel. The just, however, are fervour and fuel!

The hour when we say: 'What good is my pity! Is not pity the cross on which he is nailed who loveth man? But my pity is not a crucifixion.

Have you ever spoken thus? Have you ever cried thus? Ah! Would that I had heard you cry thus!... Lo, I teach you the Superman: he is the lightning, he is that frenzy![18]

For Nietzsche the true Superman is the one who no longer slavishly adheres to either the ethical absolutes of religion, especially a religion such as Christianity with its apparently defeated leader slaughtered on a cross as a consequence of his compassion, or the moral conventions of Enlightenment resourced modernism, an ersatz religion in its own right. Yet, while Nietzsche sees this freedom from conventional values and a radical disengagement from the other as being at the heart of his heroic Superman it would seem to me that this flies in the face of most other notions of the heroic and conforms rather more to the image of the villain.

> God hath died: now do we desire – the Superman to live ... The Superman, I have at heart; that is the first and only thing to me – and not man; not the neighbour, not the poorest, not the sorriest, not the bes t... For today have the petty people become masters; they all preach submission and humility and policy and diligence and consideration and the long et cetera of petty virtues ... Surpass, ye higher men, the petty virtues, the petty policy, the sand-grain considerateness, the ant-hill trumpery, the pitiable comfortableness, the 'happiness of the greatest number'![19]

The hero confronts the otherness of the world and seeks to overcome it, often via a willingness to set aside their unique powers thus rendering themselves vulnerable. By contrast, the villain revels in the power to control, to manipulate and ultimately to create a world in their own image. Consider one of the speeches given by 'The First', the ultimate evil faced by Buffy in the final series, to a Spike trying to come to terms with his returned soul:

> 'Look at you, trying to do what's right, just like her. You still don't get it. It's not about right, not about wrong, it's about power.'[20]

A similar distinction between the hero and the villain is made throughout George Lucas' *Star Wars* saga, where the Force – a semi-divine power – is split into two manifestations, the dark side and the light side. In the film *The Empire Strikes Back* the Jedi master Yoda explains the difference:

> YODA: A Jedi's strength flows from the Force. But beware of the dark side. Anger ... fear ... aggression. The dark side of the Force are they. Easily they flow, quick to join you in a fight. If once you start down the dark path, forever will

> it dominate your destiny, consume you it will, as it did
> Obi-Wan's apprentice.
> LUKE: Vader. Is the dark side stronger?
> YODA: No ... no ... no. Quicker, easier, more seductive.
> LUKE: But how am I to know the good side from the bad?
> YODA: You will know. When you are calm, at peace. Passive.
> A Jedi uses the Force for knowledge and defence, never for
> attack.[21]

The villain coerces, imposes and seeks to destroy anything that it cannot bend to its will. The hero takes the more dangerous path, the one that always runs the risk of self-destruction as a consequence of self-sacrifice and abandonment to the world.

In Kurt Busiek's justly praised *Astro City* comic series there is a short story simply running through the average day of the city's Superman figure, Samaritan. It opens with the words:

> In my dreams I fly. I soar unfettered and serene, laughing at
> gravity and at care. The clouds embrace me as a friend and
> the wind lazily tousles my hair. I lose myself in the sun and
> the sky.[22]

The irony is that Samaritan can actually fly. The whole story focuses upon his self sacrifice, he flies for others, never for himself. His powers are always and only at the disposal of others. 'There's no time' he thinks to himself as he flies off at super-speed to avert some disaster on the other side of the world 'There's never any time'. The story is punctuated with Samaritan pathetically timing the amount of flight time he manages during his missions:

> a lot of mid-air antics ... but its not the same as real flying.
> Four-plus hours of work ... seventeen seconds of flight. I
> deal with a runaway bus in Midtown (less than a second
> travel time) ... An attack on Denver City Hall by Dr.
> Saturday (1.1 seconds) ... and a near-disaster at FBU's bio
> labs (half a second, but only to avoid the airport ... A jail-
> break at Biro Island (less than a second to fly there) ... and
> a frightened little ball of orange and white on Cicero street. I
> slow down (two seconds) to let the little girl see me clearly

and reassure her that it's all right ... and it almost costs a man in Boston his life. I make a note to try not to waste time like that in the future.[23]

Only in his dreams is he free, free from responsibility, free to really fly.

Of course, and as Joseph Campbell observes, the hero might very well be subverted from their true path by the lure of easy power, power perhaps unearned and thus poorly understood and deployed, power without responsibility:

> if the hero, instead of submitting to all of the initiatory tests, has, like Prometheus, simply darted to his goal (by violence, quick device, or luck) and plucked the boon for the world that he intended, then the power that he has unbalanced may react so sharply that he will be blasted from within and without – crucified, like Prometheus, on the rock of his violated unconscious.[24]

It is a matter of record that George Lucas – the creator of *Star Wars* – was significantly influenced by Campbell's work. This can be plainly seen in the character of Anakin Skywalker – especially in *Episode 3* – who begins his heroic career as a Jedi Knight only to opt for the quicker and easier route to power offered by the dark side.

We see this potential danger in the Batman as he chooses between taking on the role of hero or executioner and Spiderman as he chooses the path of hero over celebrity. Ultimately it would seem that the hero, the person of power and ability, must make a choice as to whether to use their new abilities for others or for themselves so as to gain a easy advantage over others. The potential for the hero to collapse into villainy is an ever present one and hinges on the individual's sense of engagement and solidarity with the rest of the world.

The Christian religious tradition, for example, is all too familiar with this distinction between the heroic and villainous aspects of human identity. This is particularly apparent in its treatment of the human condition in its ideal and fallen sinful states.

In his book *Death: the Riddle and the Mystery*, Eberhard Jungel speaks of sin and its ultimate end in death in terms of relation-lessness. He writes:

> death is the consequence of man's pernicious drive toward this relationlessness. Man's disastrous urge towards the deadliness of relationlessness stands in direct proportion to death's aggressiveness as alienating man from God and as breaking up human relationships.[25]

In a similar vein the theologian Wolfhart Pannenberg wishes to interpret sin in terms of 'centredness' or 'ego-centricity', where the individual person's openness to God and to others is replaced by self-prioritising. Karl Barth, writing in *The Christian Life*, is quite adamant that 'the Fall' was a fall not only away from God, but away from one another: 'In and with the sin of Adam, who wanted to be as God, there is already enclosed the sin of Cain.'[26]

The Judeo-Christian picture of the Fall has at its root man's desire for autonomy and self-sufficiency. As Barth points out from the Genesis narrative, Adam's sin was that he wanted to be as God. The consequence of this dislocation from God is that we no longer consider ourselves to be our brother's keeper. Our current experience of relational brokenness prompts us always to encounter the other as a stranger. Indeed, the opening chapter of the Gospel of John illustrates how even God is now considered a stranger by us: 'He was in the world, and though the world was made through him, the world did not recognise him. He came to that which was his own, but his own did not receive him.' (John 1:10f).

Armour and isolation

It seems to me that our experience of the other as stranger is born, in part, out of fear: fear of, or at the very least anxiety over, the sin of Cain, fear of the potential for violence and animosity inherent in the mysterious stranger. It is this which represents the tragedy and paradox of relational brokenness, for while it is the mysteriousness of the stranger which fuels our fear, it is our fear which helps to fuel our estrangement from the other. This is the trap that we constantly find ourselves caught in and which the hero and the villain respond to in such dramatically different ways.

Take as an example two of Marvel comics' most enduring characters: the super hero Iron Man and the super villain Doctor Doom. Both of these characters are scientific geniuses, both have suffered severe physical damage and both have had to resort to the use of high tech armour as a result of their accidents.

Tony Stark is a rich, handsome and intelligent industrialist who gets blown-up by a landmine while demonstrating one of his inventions to the military in a war zone.[27] Stark survives the blast but his heart is fatally damaged. In order to keep his damaged heart beating Stark develops and builds a suit of armour the chest plate of which contains a sophisticated pacemaker. While for many years Stark had to wear and recharge the chest plate constantly in order to live, it was only when he donned the complete suit that he became the super powered Iron Man with enhanced strength and a range of high tech gadgets at his disposal. Along with Thor, Ant Man, The Wasp, and for a short while, the Hulk, Iron Man became one of the founder members of the Avengers, one of the most well known comic super teams of all time. However, in spite of all this Stark often agonised over his identity as Iron Man fearing that encasing himself in a metal shell would only serve to distance himself, both emotionally as well as physically, from the people he loved and those he sought to protect. At one point in his career Stark gives up being Iron Man – the role being taken on by his friend Jim Rhodes – while he himself descended into alcoholism. As he begins to recover from this period of alcohol-induced self-destruction Stark is offered his armour back:

RHODES: This is yours

STARK: Rhodey, you don't understand. I don't ever want to see that thing again. I don't want to put it on. I'm scared of it. That armour made me feel invulnerable, not like other human beings. And not being like other human beings made me a drunk. I lost my soul to a bottle, and … it's so hard to explain. Impossible to explain to someone who hasn't been there.[28]

Incidentally, the theme of alienating invulnerability is one that is taken up in the *Buffy* series in the character of the rogue vampire slayer Faith. Faith is accidentally activated as The Slayer when Buffy technically dies for a few minutes at the end of Season One. Unlike Buffy, Faith appears supremely confident, self-assured and self-contained, invulnerable in her own emotional armour. She revels in her powers and, on the face of it at least, in her isolation and studied aggressive posture towards others. When she accidentally kills a human being thinking him a vampire she crosses an important line – not the one relating to the taking of life, bad as this may be, but in her attempted justification of her actions on the basis of her superiority to the rest of humanity. It is not until we reach the final episodes of the final season that we find a repentant Faith who, like Spike, discovers her soul resides in her relationship with others.

Creating a protective shell for ourselves is one of our most valuable survival skills. We would not survive for very long in the adult world without the ability to protect our vulnerabilities, hide our feelings and project a public image. It seems to me that many of those who find it difficult to function in the world do so due to their inability to cloth themselves in the appropriate armour. However, and as Tony Stark discovers, the armour is not who we are, it is a mechanism, a means of protection and something that needs to be removed once we are no longer under threat.

While Tony Stark did eventually return to his role as Iron Man his fear of what the armour might do to his sense of self never really dissipates. The armoured villain Doctor Doom on the other hand is an entirely different matter. In *Fantastic Four Issue 5* published in 1962 Doom is introduced as a mysterious armoured genius bent on world domination. Two years later, in *Fantastic Four Annual 2*, Doom's origin is told for the first time and he is revealed to be a complex and somewhat tragic figure.

The story opens with the brooding figure of Doctor Doom being reminded of an appointment by his aged retainer Boris. The appointment is to visit the grave of his mother. We learn of Doom's humble beginnings, the violent death of his parents – often a motif in heroic fantasy, his brilliant mind and his university career where, during an experiment designed to allow him to contact his dead mother he causes an explosion which ruins his good looks and has him expelled from the institution.

Unlike Tony, Stark Doom, who was an arrogant and bitter man at best, responds to his accident by turning in on himself and shunning the rest of humanity:

> My face ... no other eyes must ever gaze upon it!! I'll hide from the sight of mankind ... somewhere ... somehow.[29]

The armour he clothes himself in is never removed and is designed to create a barrier between Doom and the rest of the world. As he dons his metal mask – still hot from the furnace, thus damaging his features further he cries:

> Never again will mortal eyes gaze upon the hideous countenance of Victor Von Doom! From this moment on, there is no Victor Von Doom! He has vanished ... along with the handsome face he once possessed! But in his place, there shall be another ... wiser, stronger! More brilliant, more powerful than ever before!! From this moment on, I shall be known as ... Doctor Doom![30]

As we mentioned earlier on in this chapter, the fact of our individual alienation from the rest of existence is something that we are forced to come to terms with. For most of us this is a condition that we are compelled to try and overcome, however this is not always the case.

The very thought of this takes me back to my teenage years when, as my adult life began to beckon, I started to realise that living in the world was a potentially painful business and raised all sorts of questions about just how vulnerable I would choose to make myself as I navigated my way through it.[31]

While it may indeed be the case that no man is an island it is equally the case that we can do a pretty good job of shutting down our borders. We can choose to armour ourselves in such a way as to both withhold ourselves from others and deny ourselves significant engagement with others. We can take our inherent alienation, our necessary transcendence from everything and everyone that is not our self, and we can choose to enhance it and feed it and make the armour what we are.

By making ourselves unavailable to the other we leave only the fact of our presence in the world, our image or armoured shell if you will.

As we have suggested, in our first encounter with the other the dominant experience is one of alienation. The other conforms to the category of stranger. Once we have assimilated the image of the other as a physical presence we are then confronted by the threatening mysteriousness of the stranger. The stranger is not mine nor is he or she *for me*, there is no availability involved in the other who is stranger; nothing of the self of the other is freely and willingly offered by the stranger. The stranger remains a stranger because they know that knowledge is power, and that to give knowledge of one self to another is to give power over oneself to the other.[32] Into the vacuum that is the stranger we empty our fears and mistrusts, casting the other in the image of the predator who is out to consume us if once given advantage over us. It is this fear which establishes estrangement as our primary experience of the other; as much as anything it is a defensive posture.

The experience of the non-availability of the stranger is, I think, universal. We need only to enter a so-called 'public' place to be able to identify the ways in which we deny ourselves to the other. Of course, the occupation of a public place is certainly a significant step towards availability in that it brings the self and the other together in proximity to each other. However, such benefits as this bestows in terms of facilitating availability can be almost completely obviated by our will towards estrangement. It is this will towards estrangement, fuelled by fear and mistrust, that will prevent two people sitting together in a doctor's waiting room from conversing with each other. We communicate nothing of ourselves in these encounters, our faces become impassive, our language monosyllabic. If we happen to be also in the company of a friend, our conversations with that person are carried out in hushed whispers.

When in a strange place I find myself loath to ask for directions for fear of placing myself in the hands of a stranger. We dread calling attention to ourselves, preferring rather the anonymity of a particular uniform, be it an office suit or denim jeans. Similarly we would rather concentrate our attentions upon anything rather than the other person: a newspaper or magazine, our mp3 player, the passing scenery or even our footwear. As strangers to the other we present only an image, a simulacra of a person. In many respects this creation of a social image acts as an isolating armour in much the same ways as does Doctor Doom's and Iron Man's referred to earlier.

Bearing in mind what we have just said concerning our experience of the other as stranger and considering this in the light of our obvious tendency towards relationships with other persons, we clearly find ourselves in the presence of a tension. The resolution of this tension is the very act of making friends. It is the transition from estrangement to communion, from the non-availability of the self to an at least partial availability. The catalyst, or catalysts, which trigger off this dramatic transition are extremely complex and it is not the task of this work to make an examination of them in any detail. However, it is relatively straightforward to catalogue some of the major factors involved. Body language has been recognised of late to play a significant part in the preliminary stages of human interaction, as have other forms of non-verbal communication such as the wearing of certain clothes, and being regularly present in certain places. Spoken language, no matter how formal the style, may also provide clues pertaining to an appropriate way into a relationship with another. A term that is sometimes used to describe these agents which catalyse relationships is sign or signal, and we shall utilise this terminology here.

A signal of availability must itself be an act of availability. By making such a signal we are communicating something of ourself to the other, albeit in a guarded way. Thus, even from within the depths of our estrangement from the other, our essential being as relational manifests itself in our first tentative offering of ourselves to the other.

As we have already mentioned, a signal of availability, whether it is active, such as wearing a badge expressing one's political persuasion, or passive, for example engaging in a piece of non-directive behaviour such as reading a book in a public place, is in itself an act of availability. Although we may fear making ourselves too available to the other and thus opening ourselves up to abuse, we cannot stop being ourselves no matter how adept we might be at rendering ourselves unavailable to the stranger. We will generally dress in a manner we find pleasing, we will read what we find interesting, we will often be found in places which we find congenial indulging ourselves in favourite pursuits. All these factors, and many others, may serve as signals indicating a non-threatening common ground upon which I and the stranger might engage.

The point of such an engagement is that while it inevitably speaks of a degree of mutual availability, it does not involve an imbalance of power. For example, in our experience of estrangement there is in operation not a dynamic of relationality but a static balance of power. I have no power over the stranger and they have no power over me. In some ways this situation may be seen as analogous to the keeping of state secrets at an international level. However once I discover, via a signal of some sort, that the stranger shares with me an appreciation of a certain type of literature, I am free to make this aspect of myself available to that person with little fear that by doing so I might be placing myself in the power of the other. For example, the person sitting next to me in the library would be unlikely to approach me as a stranger and admit to a liking for science fiction literature for fear that I might ridicule him for his interests, or simply reject this offering of personal information as a matter of complete indifference to me. However, this fear of my power to dismiss this aspect of the stranger is dissipated when the basis for the experience of this power is removed. In the light of the stranger's observation of the sign indicating my enjoyment of science fiction, he is free to offer me the same information concerning himself safe in the knowledge that sharing the same knowledge about each other gives us the same power over each other, and thus negates the potency of that power.

Of course our day-to-day experience of the stranger and our encounters with other persons are by no means as formal as the preceding comments tend to imply. However, despite this formalism, which is sadly unavoidable in any attempt at describing interpersonal relations in a systematic way, I believe the above observations to be accurate to our preliminary experience of the other, particularly as we encounter that other as stranger. I would suggest that often our fears, the transmission of signals of availability and the balancing of powers between ourselves and the stranger operate at an unconscious, instinctive level rather than at the level of cynical manipulation and out-and-out paranoia. However, the armoured isolation of villainous archetypes such as Victor Von Doom speak only of paranoia and fear of vulnerability which leaves domination as the only option for engagement with the world.

The process of developing friendship, on the other hand, takes on an heroic character as *I* continue to make myself increasing availability to and for *you*. With each new act of availability, that is, with each new reciprocal communication of an aspect of self which takes place between the self and the other, there follows a reduction in the possibility of dominating power and an increase in the power to participate. The theologian Jurgen Moltmann makes the distinction between these two modes of empowering in his 1984–1988 Gifford lectures, *God in Creation*:

> If science sets its sights on the acquisition of power, then scientific knowledge is dominating knowledge. We know something to the extent in which we can dominate it. We understand something if we can 'grasp' it … But belief in creation only arrives at the understanding of creation when it recollects the alternative forms of meditative knowledge. 'We know to the extent to which we love', said Augustine. Through this form of astonished, wondering and loving knowledge, we do not appropriate things. We recognize their independence and participate in their life. We do not wish to know so that we can dominate. We desire to know in order to participate. This kind of knowledge confers community, and can be termed communicative knowledge, as compared with dominating knowledge.[33]

With this reduction of the power to dominate the attendant fear of domination is dissipated, and is ultimately replaced by trust. The feared stranger is no more and the other has become the friend with whom I can 'feel at home'. This 'feeling at home' with another speaks of the inclusion of the other into our personal existence, home is the place where we need not wear armour. Our home is often a place where we may go and shut out the stranger; to be at home with someone is to see them not as strangers to be shut out, but as an aspect of self, and thus as participants in our lives at the most intimate of levels. To the friend we are vulnerable because when we enter our 'home' so as to shut out the rest of the world the friend is shut in with us.

Ultimately the process of signals and mutual exchanges of aspects of ourselves gives way to free communion. At this point the careful attention to the balance of power which characterises our preliminary interaction with the other is transformed by trust into unilateral self-availability. In other words, we begin to give of ourselves without the assurance of a secure power-base from which we are unassailable. We communicate with the other freely and without fear. It is for this reason that we do not have to establish a common ground, via an exchange of information, for every aspect of our lives before making it available to the other. Mature friendship does not continue as a never-ending process of mutual disarmament. There is a very real sense in which we are still potentially powerful, in a dominant way, over our friends and they over us. Friendship always involves risks precisely because as the friendship deepens, we no longer call upon our friends to divest themselves of their power over us by vouchsafing to us similar power, but rather we trust those friends not to exercise this power, which always remains theirs. It is for this reason that betrayal by a friend is the cruellest betrayal of all.

Of course, there are times when being cast in the role of the outsider or the stranger is beyond our control.

The Outsiders

While heroes such as Superman – along with all the other comic heroes who donned red, white and blue spandex, thus wrapping themselves in the flag – clearly possessed an otherness from which their power was derived, they also exhibited a fatal flaw which would ultimately compromise their transcendental impartiality – nationalism.

During the war years characters such as Superman, Wonder Woman and Captain America served as iconic symbols of the fight against fascism. In a time when the enemy was unambiguous and the threat clear and present, heroes were on the frontline destroying Hitler's war machine in Europe and smashing his spy rings at home. However, in more complicated times where the enemy was less easy to spot and sometimes dwelt 'within', the mission of the hero was far less clear cut. It was during these more cynical times that the super powered vigilante came into its own, a hero that operated outside the law and without government endorsement such that they might be able to protect us from corrupt political, corporate and bureaucratic powers that sought to dominate us covertly. If Superman is the archetype for the classic red, white and blue institutional hero then the Batman is his opposite.

the Batman, created by Bob Kane and Bill Finger and first seen in *Detective Comics 27* published in 1937, was conceived and portrayed as the archetypical vigilante. Apart from a rather unfortunate recasting in the 1960s as a less grim more establishment friendly crime fighter in the mould of Superman for the most part the Batman fought crime not for *truth, justice and the American way* but largely for revenge.

As seems to be the case with a great many heroes,[34] the Batman's heroics were catalysed by the death of his parents. The young Bruce Wayne witnesses his parents' brutal shooting during a mugging and vows to make all criminals pay.

> YOUNG BRUCE AT HIS PARENTS' GRAVESIDE: I swear I'll dedicate my life and inheritance to bringing your killer to justice … and to fighting all criminals! I swear it![35]

Incidentally, the loss of one or both parents is as much a motif in the contemporary heroic tradition as it has been in the classical mythological traditions. the Batman, Superman, Spiderman, Doctor Doom, Frodo Baggins, Luke Skywalker, Darth Vader, Buffy Summers, Harry Potter, Lyra Belacqua, and many others have all had to cope with the loss of those that loved them and cared for them from birth and who, in a less violent and less callous universe, would have been with them to support them as they grew to adulthood. This is a point made by Richard Reynolds who identifies the lost parent motif as central to the super hero make up.

> Superman is separated from his natural parents, and so his extraordinary powers are not represented in a straightforward parent-to-child relationship. Few superheroes enjoy uncomplicated relationships with parents who are regularly present in the narrative.[36]

As a millionaire – always useful in the crime fighting business – the Batman is able to devote himself to the physical and mental training necessary to conduct his war on the criminal underworld and equip himself with a staggering selection of gadgets and weapons. All of these things are necessary to young Bruce's mission as, unlike characters such as Superman or Spiderman who gained superhuman powers due to an alien heritage or scientific accident, the Batman possesses no superhuman or paranormal abilities. the Batman is one of the very few self-made comic super heroes, his abilities while formidable are nevertheless human abilities honed by obsession to their highest degree. After years of training we see Bruce Wayne as a young man sitting alone in his vast mansion brooding over his new role as vigilante, a bat flies into the room and Bruce Wayne utters some of the most memorable lines in comic history:

> Criminals are a superstitious, cowardly lot, so I must wear a disguise that will strike terror into their hearts! I must be a creature of the night, like a … a … a bat! That's it! I shall become a bat![37]

While there have been attempts to make the Batman more of a 'team player' – teaming him up with another orphan, Dick Grayson, the first Robin, having him join both the Justice League and the aptly named Outsiders[38] – the Batman is essentially a solitary figure who functions at his best alone and in the shadows.

The popularity of the Batman figure rests on a number of

important factors the most significant of which, in my view, is his sheer humanness. For all his abilities and grim detachment, Bruce Wayne's *alter ego* is driven by very human emotions to be what he is and to do what he does. His heroic actions are not, primarily, the product of lofty ideals but issue out of passion and his own pain. Loss and anger are feelings that most of us can readily associate with. We know exactly how it feels to be hurt so much we want to lash out, to feel the sense of injustice at a personal loss so intensely that we would do almost anything to put it right. While ideologies and codes of conduct and philosophies and religions may often drive a wedge between us, our common emotional experiences often serve to bind us to each other. As I write, the world is living amidst the emotional aftermath of the tsunami that devastated a large part of South-East Asia in December 2004. There is not a person I know who hasn't been touched by the pain of those most immediately caught up in this catastrophe and who doesn't wish to do something, no matter how small, about it.

The Batman carries with him the intense pain associated with the violent loss of his parents and this has prompted him to dedicate his entire life to preventing such pain occurring again, to anyone, if he can help it. His is a heroism in part generated out of empathy and made manifest in self-sacrifice.

This brings to mind an observation made by the Utilitarian philosopher John Stuart Mill who makes the following point:

> All the grand sources, in short, of human suffering are in a great degree, many of them almost entirely, conquerable by human care and effort; and though their removal is grievously slow – though a long succession of generations will perish in the breach before the conquest is completed, and this world becomes all that, if will and knowledge were not wanting, it might easily be made – yet every mind sufficiently intelligent and generous to bear a part, however small and unconspicuous, in the endeavour, will draw a noble enjoyment from the contest itself, which he would not for any bribe in the form of selfish indulgence consent to be without.

> And this leads to the true estimation of what is said by the

objectors concerning the possibility, and the obligation, of learning to do without happiness. Unquestionably it is possible to do without happiness; it is done involuntarily by nineteen-twentieths of mankind, even in those parts of our present world which are least deep in barbarism; and it often has to be done voluntarily by the hero or the martyr, for the sake of something which he prizes more than his individual happiness. But this something, what is it, unless the happiness of others or some of the requisites of happiness? It is noble to be capable of resigning entirely one's own portion of happiness, or chances of it: but, after all, this self-sacrifice must be for some end; it is not its own end; and if we are told that its end is not happiness, but virtue, which is better than happiness, I ask, would the sacrifice be made if the hero or martyr did not believe that it would earn for others immunity from similar sacrifices? Would it be made if he thought that his renunciation of happiness for himself would produce no fruit for any of his fellow creatures, but to make their lot like his, and place them also in the condition of persons who have renounced happiness? All honour to those who can abnegate for themselves the personal enjoyment of life, when by such renunciation they contribute worthily to increase the amount of happiness in the world.[39]

Of course it would be simplistic to attribute all of Bruce Wayne's behaviour to empathy and fellow feeling – our emotions are rarely if ever that un-muddied. As we mentioned earlier, unlike Superman, the Batman is as much to do with vengeance as he is to do with justice. These two driving forces, often at odds with each other, further contributes to the Dark Knight's human appeal. Who can honestly say that they haven't seen a news report concerning some senseless atrocity or other perpetrated upon the innocent by a compassionless individual and not wished that person harm? Or wished that they might be made to pay, to suffer as their victims have suffered? While the Batman generally stops short of execution – the experience of losing his parents to a callous gunman having made Bruce both value life and hate guns[40] – this does not stop him from inflicting pain and suffering upon those he considers predatory upon the weak and the innocent.

> It's tough work, carrying two hundred and twenty pounds of sociopath to the top of Gotham Towers – the highest spot in the city. The scream alone is worth it.[41]

In spite of our often professed liberal sensibilities that prompt us to speak of justice and rehabilitation and even redemption as the primary mode of dealing with criminal and anti-social individuals, the heroes of our imagination speak with a different voice. Whether it be Robin Hood finally thrusting his sword into Guy of Gisborn, or Van Helsing finally staking Count Dracula, or Luke Skywalker destroying the evil Emperor and his Death Star, or James Bond blowing up the villain in his secret lair, the effect is always the same – a rousing cheer from the audience.

The Judeo-Christian tradition speaks of vengeance being the prerogative of God[42] and this provides us with something of an insight into the popularity of heroic figures such as the Batman. There is a comfort of sorts to be found in the belief that someone out there has both the power and the ethical certainty to judge and to punish with transcendental impartiality. To be the other, to stand outside of all human conventions, to judge them equally and redress the balance of pain and suffering is indeed a divine capacity and while the Batman is certainly not a god, he fits the role of avenging angel very well indeed. In many ways the Batman is more the Nietzschean superman than is his red, white and blue counterpart who actually bears the name. While Superman is very much part of the establishment and thus never truly free to judge it, the Batman, as the other, the vigilante who stands outside established laws and conventions is free to set his own agenda to *watch the watchmen* as it were. This point is brought to a dramatic focus in Frank Miller's watershed re-establishing of the Batman's dark character in the 1986 four part mini series *Batman: The Dark Knight*. In this we encounter a Bruce Wayne in late middle age having 'retired' his Batman persona ten years earlier. Gotham city is in turmoil, the streets are owned by violent gangs, some of which are being armed with mis-appropriated military weapons, and societal infrastructures are collapsing. Into this chaotic world the Batman reappears and as his activities begin to split public opinion and unsettle the government of the day, Superman – who is now little more than a deterrent in America's arsenal – is tasked by the President to suppress him. As Superman considers how to deal with his one time ally he remembers the events leading up to the effective outlawing of super powered heroes:[43]

> SUPERMAN: You were the one they used against us Bruce. The one who played it rough. When the noise started from the parent groups and the sub-committee called us in for questioning … you were the one who laughed … that scary laugh of yours. 'Sure we're criminals,' you said. 'We've always been criminals. We have to be criminals.' We almost threw a party when you retired. By then the PBI was into it and things were getting out of hand … Do you remember why you retired, Bruce? NO … just look at you … you'd do it again … and like a murderer you'd cover it up again. Nothing matters to you except your holy war. They were considering their options and you were probably still laughing when we came to terms. I gave them my obedience and my invisibility. They gave me a licence and let us live.[44]

The eventual violent confrontation between these two iconic heroes is one of the most powerful in comic book history and highlights the essential difference between them:

> BATMAN: … and it has to end here … on this filthy patch of street … where my parents died … Still talking … keep talking Clark … you've always known just what to say. 'Yes' … you always say yes … to anyone with a badge … or a flag. You sold us out, Clark. You gave them the power … that should have been ours. Just like your parents taught you to. My parents … taught me a different lesson … lying on this street … shaking in shock … dying for no reason at all … they showed me that the world only makes sense when you force it to … We could have changed the world … now… look at us … I've become … a political liability … and you … you're a joke.[45]

Of course the difference between Superman and the Batman reflects one of the fundamental tensions within the heroic character – and brings us back to the Stan Lee quote on Spiderman referred to earlier – that between power and responsibility.

Any parent will appreciate this particular dilemma as they seek to achieve a balance between the exercise of supportive power on behalf of their children, and the often painful withdrawal of support in the interest of a child's developing autonomy. I wonder how often two parents stage the Superman/Batman struggle as one argues for the deployment of parental power only as sanctioned and requested by the child, while the other argues that it is in the child's best interest to be helped in spite of themselves? Certainly there is a time when the very young look upon their parents as almost transcendent beings possessing godlike powers of understanding and physical prowess – the ability to be able to hide behind things and to lift the child over ones head serves to establish and maintain this perception for quite some time. For a while the parent has to exercise power on behalf of the child, to paraphrase the Batman, the child's world only makes sense when it has ordered boundaries imposed upon it. Children have to be told when and what to eat, when to go to bed, what they can and cannot watch on TV, not to play with fire, not to run with scissors and how to play nicely with other children. Very young children left to their own devices would soon destroy themselves, they rely upon their parents and other adult carers to protect then and guide them – even when they are old enough to begin to resent their own lack of power and autonomy. Parents heroically sacrifice a great deal, and would gladly sacrifice a great deal more, to support and protect their children – and this without the aid of any actual superpowers. Terry Pratchett puts this rather succinctly in one of his Discworld novels 'Them as can do, has to do for them as can't. And someone has to speak up for them as has no voice.'[46]

It might be argued that the true test of the heroic is whether one is prepared to sacrifice the role. When the parent is no longer required to provide controlling support to their children, when they are requested to 'retire' from that role so that the child may take responsibility for their own lives and make their own mistakes, this is a hard thing. It seems to me that just as with the Batman, the temptation is always there to return, to look upon the mess that our loved ones may be making of their lives and to intervene. Of course the difference between intervention and interference is both a fine one and one of perspective.

How we recognise when it is appropriate to become involved in the lives of others, and when it is not, is a complicated life skill that I don't believe we ever fully master. The tragedy is that it is often only from the point of view of the outsider that the true nature of another's predicament becomes apparent, however it is equally the case that one's very status as an outsider militates against ever being asked to help.

The hero is often left with two choices; to force their aid upon others, on the dangerous assumption that they know better, or to stand back and respect the others' free will come what may. Elsewhere I have considered the political out-workings of this issue drawing on the genre of science fiction as a way of focusing the debate.[47] There we raised the issue of superior power being allied with a sense of moral superiority. At the time of writing that piece, NATO's military action in former Yugoslavia was drawing to a close, as I write this, American and British forces continue to be heavily committed in the Gulf. Putting aside questions concerning the underlying motivations for these military incursions the question remains, does any individual or country have the moral right to intervene in another's affairs by virtue of perceived moral superiority and overwhelming force?

Aeon Skoble makes this point in connection with Frank Miller's *Dark Knight* revision of the Batman:

> For Batman, the presence of a badge or a flag is neither necessary nor sufficient for justice. Laws may be unjust, politicians may be corrupt, and the legal system may act-ually protect the wicked, but none of this will deter Batman from his mission. The crime-fighting vigilante superhero does not let anything stand between him and the attainment of what he sees as real justice. Why should well-meaning social structures be allowed to stand in the way of what is objectively right?

> This can all seem to make some degree of sense, provided
> that the vigilante is in fact doing good, but it would be far
> more troubling if vigilantes lack a clear perception of right
> and wrong.[48]

While one might see no problem in preventing two young
children from harming themselves by stepping in and physically
separating them, and while we may similarly feel justified in
intervening between two older children brawling in the street,
we begin to hesitate when two adults are involved. This maybe,
at some level, be due to fear for our own safety but even if that
weren't an issue – let's say we are speaking of two small and
unintimidating individuals in this case – we would, I believe, be
inclined to the opinion that it was none of our business. So how
does this work out in the context of international relations? The
notion of a shared humanity or an absolute ethic, or even something more formal and consensual such as international law,
would seem to suggest that there are no boundaries that cannot
be crossed in the name of justice and yet, can an enforced freedom, a Utopia founded upon the threat of a putative use of
power ever be fully justified? In the comic series significantly
entitled *The Authority* Warren Ellis poses this very question by
taking the notion of the vigilante superhero team to its logical
conclusion. *The Authority* – clearly based upon Superman and
Batman's own *Justice League of America* – have no compunction
about killing any number of their opponents with extreme prejudice. Jenny Sparks, the team leader, has this to say as she uses her
power to electrocute dozens of opponents floundering in the
Thames:

> Morning, you murdering scumbags. My name is Jenny
> Sparks. I'm electricity. I'm a hundred years old and I've
> never hated anyone as much as you. This is my bloody town
> you tried to kill. And you're getting only what you
> deserve.[49]

This unrestrained power in the service of an uncompromising
moral code culminates in the Authority taking on god-like
responsibility for world order across a number of alternative
Earths. In Jenny's final speech to one such Earth, from the

Authority's headquarter which appropriately exists in a trans-cendental dimension between all worlds, she makes her team's agenda perfectly clear:

> This is Jennifer Sparks for the Authority. Albion is free of the Blue. Sicily and the Italian capital infrastructure are gone. If need be we can annihilate the Hanseatic regions within the hour. If we are asked to, we will go into China and Japan. If we have to, we will personally expunge the royal blood and military rape culture from the face of the planet. We're here to give you a second chance. Make a world worth living in. We are the Authority. Behave.[50]

This theme is explored in the 2006 Marvel Comic mini-series *Civil War* written by Mark Miller, where the world's heroes are divided over the issue of government registration. Should these powerful individuals be accountable to the state or function out-side trusting to their own sense of what is right and wrong to govern their actions?

Captain America is called to an intelligence meeting where he is asked to comment on the superheroic community's reaction to the proposed registration bill:

> AGENT HILL: This proposal goes to a vote in two weeks' time and could be law in as little as a month. But we can't go in half-cocked. We're already developing an anti-super-human response unit here, but we need to make sure the Avengers are onside and that you're out there leading the Avengers.
>
> CAPTAIN AMERICA: Forget about it. You're asking me to arrest people who risk their lives for this country every day of the week.
>
> AGENT HILL: No, I'm asking you to obey the will of the American people, Captain.
>
> CAPTAIN AMERICA: Don't play politics with me, Hill. Super heroes need to stay above that stuff or Washington starts telling us who the super-villains are.
>
> AGENT HILL: I thought super-villains were guys in masks who refused to obey the law.[51]

As we have seen, the extent to which we isolate ourselves from the world, the nature of the barriers that we erect to protect ourselves from pain and harm may be seen as having a direct influence upon our heroic or villainous tendencies. While being open to the other, the stranger, may indeed put us at risk shielding ourselves too effectively from such risk may very well leave us indifferent to others, surely one of the first steps towards villainy?

We all possess power of some sort or another, how and when we use it is the issue that confronts us and to a significant degree can mark us out as either hero or villain.

In the next chapter we will consider this relationship between heroes, villains and power.

3

With Great Power Comes Great Responsibility

> Of the infinite desires of man, the chief are the desires for power and glory.[1]

To say that a hero has to wield power would seem, on the face of it anyway, to be a rather obvious statement to make. What, after all, is the point of a powerless hero? Yet, the nature of power and how it is deployed is a complex issue that can appear to collapse into paradox when even apparent powerlessness becomes powerful. But we are ahead of ourselves here.

In his famous study of power – particularly of power that human beings exert over each other – Bertrand Russell attempts to define it in this way:

> Power may be defined as the production of intended effects. It is thus a quantitative concept: given two men with similar desires, if one achieves all the desires that the other achieves, and also others, he has no more power than the other. But there is no exact means of comparing the power of two men of whom one can achieve one group of desires, and another another; e.g. given two artists of whom each wishes to paint good pictures and become rich, and of whom one succeeds in painting good pictures and the other in becoming rich, there is no way of estimating which has the more power. Nevertheless, it is easy to say, roughly, that A has more

power than B, if A achieves many intended effects and B only a few.[2]

At its most basic level power could be seen as simply the ability to effect change, to be able to manipulate – for good or ill – the world in which we find ourselves. In this regard, and as we mentioned at the end of the last chapter, we can all be said to have power. The simple fact of our being in the world creates a myriad of changes and alterations to the world which manipulate and redefine it on a variety of subtle levels. Sheer existence itself constitutes a power, that we *are* at all is, in many ways, our most compelling and significant power. We often speak of being in the right place at the right time as having the effect of enhancing our powers and abilities; placing us at an advantage and yet, it seems to me, being in any place at any time is not without its own unique power.

Take for example the 1946 film *It's a Wonderful Life* in which a disillusioned and suicidal George Bailey considers his – apparently – unremarkable life. As he comes to the conclusion that his life is valueless and prepares to end it by throwing himself into the river, divine forces intervene and an angelic being is sent to rescue him:

GEORGE: I found it out a little late. I'm worth more dead than alive.

CLARENCE: Now look, you mustn't talk like that. I won't get my wings with that attitude. You just don't know all that you've done. If it hadn't been for you …

GEORGE: Yeah, if it hadn't been for me, everybody'd be a lot better off. My wife, and my kids and my friends. (*annoyed with Clarence*) Look, little fellow, go off and haunt somebody else, will you?

CLARENCE: No, you don't understand. I've got my job …

GEORGE: Aw, shut up, will you.

CLARENCE: Hmmm, this isn't going to be so easy. So you still think killing yourself would make everyone feel happier, eh?

GEORGE: Oh, I don't know. I guess you're right. I suppose it would have been better if I'd never been born at all.

CLARENCE: What'd you say?
GEORGE: I said I wish I'd never been born.[3]

George is granted his hasty wish and lives, for a short time, in a world in which he had never before existed. In this George-less world – perhaps overly emphasised for effect – all is not well. The many people whose lives George touched for the better, now lack that encounter and all that it gave birth to. George wasn't there to save his younger brother from drowning, and consequently as his brother never grew up to be a fighter pilot during the Second World War, and thus was never in a position to save a troop carrier, thousands perished. A young woman who should have been saved from a life of prostitution by George is now seen plying her trade outside of a local bar. The pharmacist who was prevented by George from accidentally poisoning a customer due to a momentary lapse of concentration during a moment of grief, is seen as a ruined man shunned by society for the fatal mistake that in this world actually occurred. These are just some of the many – and it has to be said only the positive – examples of the power of an individual existence that George Bailey is made to confront before he realises that, in spite of never having travelled the world or performed obviously great and heroic deeds, he has lived a wonderful life and he wants it back.[4]

If existential philosophers such as Jean-Paul Sartre teach us anything at all it is about the power of human existence and that it is *without excuse*. In a characteristically bleak section from his *Being and Nothingness* Sartre makes this none the less important point, germane, I think, to George Bailey's predicament:

> I am without excuse; for from the instant of my uprising into being, I carry the weight of the world by myself alone without anything or any person being able to lighten it.
>
> Yet this responsibility is of a very particular type. Someone will say, 'I did not ask to be born.' This is a very naïve way of throwing greater emphasis on our facticity. I am responsible for everything … I am abandoned in the world, not in the sense that I might remain abandoned and passive in a hostile universe like a board floating on the water, but rather in the sense that I find myself suddenly

alone and without help, engaged in a world for which I bear the whole responsibility without being able, whatever I do, to tear myself away from this responsibility for an instant … To make myself passive in the world, to refuse to act upon things and upon Others is still to choose myself, and suicide is one mode among others of being-in-the-world.[5]

Rather dark perhaps but a valuable observation for all that. Being-in-the-world, no matter how one does it, involves us in responsibility and choice and for every choice we make we exert power in some way. Even, as Sartre points out, being passive, avoiding active decision making, collapsing into apathy, even in these we are still making a choice, we are still effecting the world. It's a bit like the old adage that not voting is effectively a vote for the *status quo*. Our lives always matter.

Of course, typically, the hero is not one who is characterised by inactivity and lack of involvement in the world. More often than not the heroic deployment of power is both proactive and clearly focused. Heroes – and villains for that matter – are a goal orientated breed as is amply attested to by the vast array of heroic quests we find within the relevant media. The hero is endlessly engaged in rescuing, defending, seeking and overcoming.[6] Yet, in spite of the general uniformity of mission parameters the hero can be seen to have a variety of modes of power at their command; not every hero, for example, makes use of enhanced physical strength and martial arts prowess to deal with their enemies. While hitting things until they fall over or break is indeed an approach much favoured by the classic hero, this is by no means the only form of engagement that we may identify. Power, as we mentioned above, comes in many forms.

In Paul Dini and Alex Ross's graphic novel *The World's Greatest Super-Heroes* classic heroes such as Superman and Batman are portrayed as confronting ordinary human suffering rather than the usual array of super villains. The Superman story paints a sobering picture of human poverty and greed as our hero sets himself the task of addressing world hunger. He finally concludes that in spite of all his power his mission is a failure:

As you know, I have always tried to provide comfort for

those in want, pain and fear. Many times I'd considered taking stronger action to help the world, but realized such measures could be short sighted and disastrous. I tried to relieve world hunger, but I encountered heartbreaking poverty, not only in the slums and wastelands of the world but within selfish men's souls. I now see that taking on this responsibility was too ambitious for one man, even a Superman ... if there is a solution to the problem of hunger, it must be one that comes from the compassionate heart of man and extends outward towards his fellow man.[7]

... to take up arms against a sea of troubles

Like it or not, it would seem that coercive power, the use of force, is very much part of the heroic make up. It is not just the villain who is seen to indulge in violence to achieve goals, many heroes are certainly not averse to fighting fire with fire. However, to what extent it might be legitimate to exercise coercive power in the name of goodness, justice and the heroic ideal is a very serious question. In the fight against evil and villainy is there ever room for the limiting statement 'this we do not do'?

In Tolkien's epic *Lord of the Rings* we encounter one of the starkest representations of the use and abuse of power in contemporary heroic literature. Throughout much of the story the forces of evil, symbolised in the demonic unseen figure of the dark lord Sauron, are portrayed as overwhelming. The plight of the good and the noble of Middle Earth – be they great elven lords or ordinary hobbit gardeners – seems all but beyond hope. Dark armies roam the lands murdering, pillaging and destroying. The evil of Sauron and his forces is depicted as utterly irredeemable, from his nine Nazgul lieutenants to the lowliest of Orc foot soldiers. There is never any suggestion that negotiations could be entered into or that compromises could be reached. It would be difficult to conceive of Gandalf, Aragorn, Saruman and Sauron sitting round the table trying to work out their differences. The only response to unmitigated evil here seems to be force, the exercise of power – and of course a covert black-op mission behind enemy lines.

However, in the face of an almost insurmountable evil the forces of good stop short of utilising 'the One Ring', the weapon of the enemy. While the Ring is clearly understood to be a weapon of incredible power – certainly enough to overthrow Sauron and end the present war – the cost of making use of such a resource is considered, by most, to be far too great. This is made quite clear when Boromir of the beleaguered city of Gondor suggests that the ring ought to be used in its defence:

> 'Alas, no,' said Elrond. 'We cannot use the Ruling Ring. That we now know too well. It belongs to Sauron and was made by him alone, and is altogether evil. Its strength, Boromir, is too great for anyone to wield at will, save only those who have already a great power of their own. But for them it holds an even deadlier peril. The very desire of it corrupts the heart. Consider Saruman. If any of the Wise should with this Ring overthrow the Lord of Mordor, using his own arts, he would then set himself on Sauron's throne, and yet another Dark Lord would appear ... as long as it is in the world it will be a danger even to the Wise. Nothing is evil in the beginning. Even Sauron was not so. I fear to take the ring to hide it. I will not take the ring to wield it.'[8]

This is a common motif in heroic narratives, the hero's abhorrence of the weapons and methods of evil. That the hero might so easily fall to the dark through the embracing of tainted tools and powers is a constant threat to those whose calling is often to confront foes more obviously powerful and less constrained by morality. Boromir's collapse into momentary madness where he seeks to seize the One Ring from Frodo, so as to carry it away to his city of Gondor, is in many respects a very human madness we can all comprehend. Most of us, I think, would be prepared to risk a great deal in the defence of those whom we love, indeed it is not uncommon for a sort of madness to come upon us at such times. Considering the tragic character of Boromir I am forced to wonder what wild and reckless course I would be prepared to embark upon in order to protect the ones I love, what terrible things I would be prepared to do, what anonymous others I would be prepared to compromise just so long as I could save those nearest and dearest to me. More worryingly, I wonder what I would be capable of if I possessed the power to render myself immune from retribution.

In *The Republic* Plato – through the character of Glaucon – explores this issue by telling the story of Gyges a simple shepherd who also discovers a magic ring of invisibility.

> Having made his discovery he managed to get himself included in the party that was to report to the king, and when he arrived seduced the queen, and with her help attacked and murdered the king and seized the throne.
>
> Imagine now that two such rings existed and the just man put on one, the unjust the other. There is no one, it would commonly be supposed, who would have such iron strength of will as to stick to what is right and keep his hands from taking other people's property. For he would be able to steal from the market whatever he wanted without fear of detection, to go into any man's house and seduce anyone he liked, to murder or release from prison anyone he felt inclined, and generally behave as if he had supernatural powers. And in all this the just man would differ in no way from the unjust ...[9]

In the second of the *Star Trek* films an heroic Mr Spock sacrifices his life for the good of the rest of the crew of the *Enterprise* asserting, in characteristic logical mode and with his dying breath, that *the needs of the many outweigh the needs of few or the one*. In the third film, where it has been ascertained that Spock has in some way survived, the rather more impulsive Admiral Kirk goes in search of his friend putting himself and others in jeopardy – and losing the *Enterprise* – countering Spock's utilitarian statement in the previous film with his own variant, *the needs of the few outweigh the needs of the many*. While certainly not logical, Kirks passionate concern for his friend, at the expense of almost every other consideration is easily understood. It is both the greatest power and potentially the greatest weakness of the hero to love and care and strive beyond reason. The hero is the one who turns back and waits for their injured friend knowing that the hordes of the enemy are close on their heels, the one who stands alone on the bridge barring the progress of an overwhelming foe in order to allow their companions time to escape, the one who refuses to take one innocent life as a means to saving thousands. The hero is the one who returns to an alien infested space ship, set to self-destruct in minutes, to save the cat.

There is an existential immediacy about the way in which the hero engages with the world. While concerns about humanity and the fate of nations and worlds as a whole are indeed an issue, this rarely seems to get in the way of the hero's concern for the individual and the particular. To violate the sanctity of an individual life for the sake of some grand and abstract plan – no matter how noble – is generally regarded as one of the weapons of the enemy.[10]

In George Lucus's *Star Wars* series of films we are told of the Force, an ill-defined cosmic energy that is generated by all life in the universe and which can be called upon to serve specially trained individuals – principally the Jedi Knights. The Force has two aspects, a dark and a light side. As we saw in the previous chapter, the dark side is seen as *Quicker, easier, more seductive*[11] and it is this easy power, sought out in the first instance in the cause of good, that eventually tempts the young Jedi Knight Anakin Skywalker and ultimately redefines him as the sinister Jedi Darth Vader.[12]

In Michael Moorcock's classic Elric saga the anti-hero Elric of Melniboné, the albino ruler of the decadent city of Imrryr, requires a regular intake of drugs to maintain his strength and well being. However, on retrieving one of the ancient rune swords, Stormbringer, he enters into a strange symbiotic relationship with the weapon which he soon discovers to be a sentient being. The sword, it would seem, feeds on the souls of those it slays and passes on the strength and vitality of its victims to Elric who no longer requires sorcerous drugs to sustain him. Elric often fights to protect the innocent and for heroic ideals and yet, without his vampiric sword and the power it bestows upon him he would be weak and ineffectual. A pact with the devil indeed.

> Elric felt fresh energy pour up his right arm and into his body. This was what the sword could do. With it, he needed no drugs, would never be weak again. In battle he would

triumph. At peace, he could rule with pride. When he travelled, it could be alone and without fear …

And what must the sword have in return?

Elric knew. The sword told him, without words of any sort. Stormbringer needed to fight, for that was its reason for existence. Stormbringer needed to kill, for that was its source of energy, the lives and souls of men, demons – even gods.[13]

The transition from hero to villain due to the inappropriate use of power and dubious methods is, I would suggest, usually a gradual process and one that is not generally noticed until it is too late. Justifying the application of violent power towards the innocent in the name of a higher cause is a common enough strategy among the worlds leaders. Whether it manifests itself economically via redundancies, or socially via the reduction in public services, or militarily in the bombing of civilians so as to bring down a tyrannical government, the decision is taken that innocent individuals must suffer for the greater good. The question is, can one ever balance such an equation? Is one life actually less important than two lives in any meaningful sense?

Of course, the simple fact of the matter is that in the battle against evil and villainy people are going to get hurt, heroes and villains fall and innocent bystanders are caught in the cross fire. Worst of all, at the end of the day, evil is never seen to be conclusively defeated, only its current manifestation is suppressed, and the conflict goes on merely with a change of venue.

Epic battles and force of arms are clearly at the heart of the heroic story. The hero fights for those who cannot fight for themselves, fights against all hope, fights even against all reason when there is no obvious way to win. Part of what attracts us to the hero is their strength, their ability to stand up to evil and villainy, to beat it back or sometimes just to stand in its way. In the Season Three episode of *Buffy the Vampire Slayer*, 'Gingerbread', where the whole town of Sunnydale appears up in arms over the death of two small children, Buffy speaks with her estranged lover, Angel:

BUFFY: My mom … said some things to me about being the Slayer. That it's fruitless. No fruit for Buffy.

> ANGEL: She's wrong.
>
> BUFFY: Is she? Is Sunnydale any better than when I first came here? Okay, so I battle evil. But I don't really win. The bad keeps coming back and getting stronger.
>
> ANGEL: Buffy, you know, I'm still figuring things out. There's a lot I don't understand. But I do know it's important to keep fighting. I learned that from you.
>
> BUFFY: But we never …
>
> ANGEL: We never win.
>
> BUFFY: Not completely.
>
> ANGEL: We never will. That's not why we fight. We do it 'cause there's things worth fighting for.[14]

The old adage 'all that is required for evil to flourish is for good people to do nothing' would seem to express a fundamental truth about the nature of our world. Sadly it would seem, and all things being equal, humanity does tend towards the dark side. We fear punishment and censure but more often than not it is law rather than conscience that keeps us in check. Fear of getting caught is frequently what keeps our baser instincts under control. However, with increased power comes a concomitant increase in our invulnerability, or at the very least our perceived invulnerability, to both physical and, regrettably, legal force. In commenting upon ex-US President Richard Nixon's involvement in the so-called Watergate political scandal the Christian ethicist Stanley Hauerwas makes this insightful observation:

> one of the great ironies of our society is that by attempting to make freedom an end in itself we have become an excessively legalistic society. As Solzhenitsyn points out, we feel there is little need for voluntary self-restraint, as we are free to operate to the limit of the law. Thus in condemning Richard Nixon, virtues of decency and honesty were invoked, but the legal system offered the only code by which the unacceptableness of those actions could be clearly and cogently expressed.[15]

It seems to me that a point is inevitably reached when an individual, or group of individuals, no longer feel themselves answerable to the laws, conventions, traditions and taboos of society and thus feel free to act without conscience in the world.

One of the most basic manifestations of this can be seen in the school bully who, perhaps by virtue of above average physical size or charisma, is able to intimidate their peers. Indeed, eventually reputation alone becomes enough of a power to induce fear and to dominate others. Part of the power of the villain, as we shall see later, is to do the unthinkable, to be capable of performing acts that fall outside of both conscience and law. These are the sort of acts that make the rest of us wonder 'What kind of person could do such a thing?' When confronting such individuals or regimes it is hard to think of a response short of physical force and restraint that might contain them.

Just war

In the so called 'war against terror' that followed on from the attack on the United States on 11 September 2001 debates concerning the appropriate use of force have become of particular relevance. In attempting to legitimate the use of violent force as a method of confronting a perceived evil the notion of the just war has often deployed, an approach that has had a significant impact upon the Christian theological tradition – especially Catholicism – through thinkers such as Augustine and Aquinas.

> The real evils in war are love of violence, revengeful cruelty, fierce and implacable enmity, wild resistance, and the lust for power, and such like; and it is generally to punish these things, when force is required to inflict the punishment, that in obedience to God or some lawful authority, good men undertake wars, when they find themselves in such a position as regards the conduct of human affairs, that right conduct requires them to act, or to make others act in this way.[16]

What Augustine has to say concerning just war is scattered throughout his famous work *The City of God* and also the *Reply to Faustus the Manichaean*. However, it is generally held that eight principles can be drawn for these sources:

1. The only cause for a just war is in response to violent aggression.

2. The only intention of such action is to restore peace and any violated rights.
3. War must always be a last resort after all other courses of action have failed.
4. A war may only be deemed just if it is legally sanctioned by the highest authority.
5. A just war needs to be focused upon clearly defined goals. Waged just so long as is necessary to restore justice and neutralize aggression. The evil done by waging such a war must not outweigh the good being sought by such extreme measures.
6. The means used to wage such a war must be proportional to the offence and the desired end.
7. Combatants must seek to distinguish between civilian and legitimate military targets.
8. There must be a reasonable chance of winning the war.[17]

While these are undoubtedly very laudable ideals the sad fact of the matter is that they are proving to be increasingly naïve with respect to the armed conflicts of the present day – indeed some would argue that they were never anything else.

Questions such as the nature of violent aggression, the definition of human rights, what constitutes legitimate authority, who is in a position to establish realistic goals for armed conflict and where one draws the line between the civilian and the military are complex ones which are not easily resolved. Furthermore, issues relating to civil conflict and rebellion against ones own leaders muddy the waters further.

The conflict between Sauron and the free people of Middle Earth, for example, is presented as an ideological one, a clash of world views, and in such a conflict there is no room for any kind of truce or any set of rules governing behaviour as there is seldom – if ever – any common ground upon which to establish such things. This is made abundantly clear in Saruman's conversation with Gandalf:

> The Younger Days are beginning. The time of the Elves is over, but our time is at hand: the world of Men, which we must rule. But we must have power, power to order all

things as we will, for that good which only the Wise can see
… A new Power is rising. Against it the old allies and policies will not avail us at all. There is no hope left in Elves or
dying Numenor. This then is one choice before you, before
us. We may join with that Power. It would be wise, Gandalf.
There is hope that way. Its victory is at hand; and there will
be rich reward for those that aid it. As the Power grows, its
proved friends will also grow; and the Wise, such as you and
I, may with patience come at last to direct its course, to control it. We can bide our time, we can keep our thoughts in
our hearts, deploring maybe evils done by the way, but
approving the higher and ultimate purpose: Knowledge,
Rule, Order; all the things we have so far striven in vain to
accomplish, hindered rather than helped by our weak or idle
friends. There need not be, any real change in our designs,
only in our means.[18]

This last sentence may very well sound all manner of ethical
alarms that, as we saw in the previous chapter, the likes of
Immanuel Kant sought to install for us. Committing evil for the
sake of a hoped for greater good, and using others as a means to
this end, is a dangerous procedure and fraught with peril. There
is a fundamental flaw at the centre of Saruman's thinking – as
reflected in his speech above – and it is one that ultimately
contributes to both his destructive excesses and his eventual
undoing. Saruman, it would seem, mistakes ideological commitment for genuine prediction. This is often the case with those
who assume a metaphysical mandate for their actions and it is, I
believe, potentially one of the most dangerous errors that can be
made by those who wield power. To justify the use of force on the
grounds that God is in some way 'on our side' or that we occupy
'the moral high ground' or that we have some manner of unique,
transcendental insight into the nature of things denied lesser
mortals, too often leads to totalitarianism of one kind or another.
History, it would seem, is full of villainous butchers who thought
themselves to be on a spiritual mission or holy crusade. Indeed,
it is not just evil political or military despots who are susceptible
to this kind of thinking, it has proved to be a problem for many
high minded and otherwise virtuous philosophers, particularly

those of an idealist persuasion such as Plato and Fichte and Hegel.

The observation that Plato's celebrated Republic, with its ordered society based upon metaphysical ideals, ultimately collapses into totalitarianism is a common place one. However, these totalistic themes identifiable within the work of this architect of western idealist philosophy were sadly repeated within the eighteenth and early nineteenth centuries by thinkers such as Johann Gottlieb Fichte (1762–1814) and Georg Wilhelm Friedrich Hegel (1770–1831) and, it could be argued, to disastrous effect for the early part of the twentieth century.

The universal vs the particular

This is not, you will be pleased to hear, the place to go into either Fichte or Hegel's particular forms of idealism in any detail. Suffice it to say that both thinkers understood the particular and the individual as merely alienated aspects of a greater metaphysical whole, an absolute spirit or consciousness. In Hegel at the very least, this absolute spirit could be understood in a pantheistic way. The impact of this upon human history manifests itself in the idea that the state or certain civilizations represent the almost incarnate manifestation of this absolute mind or spirit.

Fichte, for example, absolutising the general will, the state, by virtue of its being a contractually limited finite manifestation of the absolute mind or will, effectively argues that there exists a metaphysical mandate for both enforced conformity to the state, and also totalitarian expansionism directed at those functioning outside of the authentic rational state. In other words, by investing the German nation with this mandate, by giving it an almost divine status, Fichte could certainly be seen as at least contributing to the foundational ideology of Nazism – although we must take care not to lapse into convenient but sloppy scapegoatism.

Fichte, following in the footsteps of Kant, exhibits a similar attitude towards military expansionism as did the neo-Kantians. He maintains in his *Grundzuge*, that 'It is the natural tendency of every civilized state to widen its borders on every side and to take up all available territory into its own civic unity.' R. H. Murray has highlighted the way in which Fichte took the law-giver of Rousseau and turned him into Nietzsche's Superman:

> Anticipating both Carlyle and Nietzsche, Fichte writes: 'To compel man to adopt the rightful form of government, to impose Right on them by force, is not only the right, but the sacred duty of every man who has both the insight and the power to do so. There may even be circumstances in which the single man has this right' – a Herr Hitler, for instance – 'against the whole of mankind; for, as against him and Right, there is no man who has either rights or liberty. He may compel them to Right that being an absolutely definite conception, valid for all men alike; a conception which they all ought to have and which they all will have as soon as they raise themselves to his level of intelligence, and which, in the meantime, thanks to the grace of God working in him, he holds in the name of all and as their representative. The truth of this conception he must take upon his own conscience. He, we may say, is the compulsive power, ordained of God.[19]

In his Address to the German Nation, Fichte exhorts the German people to unify in the face of Napoleon, to become the custodians of the Right and to promulgate it via their patriotic zeal. Continuing along these lines we find him exhorting the virtues of the dictator. He argues that only such a Hero may save men from their own follies:

> The only check assumed by the hero or dictator is the tender mercies of his own conscience ... the dictator is the very man to coerce warring wills into one, and so hasten the progress of mankind. Force and right, according to Joubert, are the governors of this world; force till right is ready – la force en attendant le droit. Fichte remembered force, and forgot right.[20]

In the work of Hegel we can see a very similar tendency. Although we might wish to take a cooler line than some of his more vitriolic critics[21] it is hard to see how a system which teaches the logical necessity of the domination of the one over the many could avoid an accusation of totalism. Hegel does indeed invest the state with considerable authority, encouraging conflicts between states as a means of stimulating the development of the Freedom of Spirit as developing throughout history. Bertrand Russell makes this point when he writes of Hegel:

> In external relations ... the State is an individual, each State is independent as against others ... He goes on to argue against any sort of League of Nations by which the independence of separate States might be limited ... Conflicts of States can only be decided by war ... Their rights have their reality in their particular wills and the interest of each State is its highest law.[22]

Such a view, argues Russell, serves to justify 'every internal tyranny and every external aggression that can possibly be imagined'. In statements such as 'But the universal, that is to say the state, government, and law, is the permanent underlying mean in which the individuals and their satisfaction have and receive their fulfilled reality, inter-mediation, and persistence'.[23] Hegel does indeed appear to glorify the state. The state is not simply a mechanism for the protection of individual properties – as John Locke would have it – but rather a transcendent entity which demands and has the right to the life of any citizen. In this sense the state is seen as practically divine. Consequently Hegel regards war as a worthwhile necessity insofar as it strengthens the state, preventing stagnation and the development of private interest.[24]

This divinisation of the state is one that has been depicted powerfully in all its villainous disregard for human individuality and dignity in George Orwell's classic novel *Nineteen Eighty-Four*. While it is the character of O'Brien who acts as the voice of the state, it is the state symbolised by 'Big Brother' that is the true villain of the piece. While interrogating the hapless Winston Smith – who represents individual human identity – O'Brien expresses the essence of Orwell's concerns over the prioritising of the state over its individual members:

'Does Big Brother exist?'

'Of course he exists. The Party exists. Big Brother is the embodiment of the Party.'

'Does he exist in the same way as I exist?'

'You do not exist' said O'Brien.[25]

In support of this view of the state Hegel also develops a notion of history as the process by which the Spirit comes to its own self-consciousness. In this we might plot the 'path' of the Spirit as it proceeds throughout history leaving in its wake the great civilizations of the world.

The progression of the Spirit takes the form of a linear development from east to west beginning with the civilization of China and India, moving steadily on through Greece and Rome and finally to the Germanic races. Never again will the Spirit retrace its steps claims Hegel, and thus the oriental peoples will never progress any further than the level of infancy at which they were left when the Spirit moved on. Each newly visited civilization is greater and more advanced than the one preceding it, for these past historical phenomena were the manifestation of the Spirit growing in self-awareness and freedom.[26]

It will come as little surprise to find that for Hegel, as we saw in Fichte, the final destination of the Spirit, the point at which it manifests itself as truly mature, truly free is within the Germanic civilization of his day. Germany, says Hegel, is the final expression of the Spirit and as such has a divine duty to disseminate its culture by whatever means seems appropriate. For this reason R. H. Murray lays this accusation at Hegel's door:

> 'Die Welt-Geschichte ist das Welt-Gericht', was the view of Schiller. The history of the world is the judgement of the world. Hegel adapted it to mean that the history of the world is the supreme court at whose bar each nation stands incessantly to plead for life or death. He himself stands at the bar of this court, and his supreme condemnation is that it is he, more than Kant or even Fichte, who bestowed upon the German that sense of a divine mission of the State which the modern world witnesses with dismay.[27]

It was against the great totalising systems of Hegel and his like that the Christian existentialist Søren Kierkegaard set himself, reasserting the importance of individual personal choice. Similarly, but from an entirely other direction, Nietzsche also took issue with Hegelian absolutism and, it could be argued, provided the basis for postmodernism's rejection of grand or meta-narratives. If nothing else postmodernism, in all its various forms, teaches us to be wary of absolute confidence in our ability to transcend the world and see 'the big picture'. While there may indeed be such a picture, a single truth, a right way to see the world, our ability to access such a perspective must be constantly brought into question. As Gandalf argues with Frodo who had just offered the opinion that Gollum deserves death:

> Deserves it! I dare say he does. Many that live deserve death. And some that die deserve life. Can you give it to them? Then do not be too eager to deal out death in judgement. For even the very wise cannot see all ends.[28]

To make callous use of the other, to utilise violent force in the service of some apparent higher principle or power is a dubious and perilous procedure at best. Just how far ahead can we really see? What, exactly are the limits of our horizons? How far do we exert control even over own personal lives? I may well be able to predict with some certainty that I will make myself a cup of tea in the next five minutes, I might even confidently state that I am going to have fish for tea tonight but can I really make any certain predictions about what I may have for breakfast tomorrow? If we lack even the vantage point to be able to make trivial predictions of this nature how safe are we in making judgments concerning the ultimate future benefits of a present act of violence against another?

Means and ends

This of course is the essence of the long running debate between so called deontological and teleological ethics. The first of these argues, along with Kant for example, that as we never have the point of view necessary to make predictions concerning the outcome of our actions we must be constrained by an absolute system of ethics. In other words, what we *ought to do* is never mitigated by circumstance or by any apparent insight into possible repercussions. So, just as we saw with Buffy in the previous chapter, taking an innocent life, even in the almost certain knowledge that not to do so may very well bring about a greater evil, is never an option. The reason for this having to do, at least in part, with the two words *almost* and *may*. On the other hand, a teleological ethicist would argue that life is far to complex to be governed by a set of inflexible rules and that the uniqueness of each situation ought to influence our ethical response.

Imagine, if you will, a mad axe-man is chasing you down the street. You duck round a corner and manage to hide in a nearby skip as a passer-by looks on. The axe-man turns the corner and upon seeing the passer-by asks them if they have seen you. Now, a teleological ethicist would advise that the passer-by ought, quite reasonably, to lie and say that they have seen no one. The deontological ethicist, on the other hand, is quite likely to argue that telling a lie is always wrong and thus perhaps the passer-by ought really to point you out. Now while this might sound ridiculously harsh it could be argued that as we cannot predict the future we cannot know what the eventual outcome of any course of action might be. To lie to the axe-man might very well lead to him embarking upon a mad killing spree to vent his frustration at not finding you. Having been directed to your hiding place and dispatching you in his chosen manner his murderous rage may well dissipate and he may abandon his rampage and give himself up to the police.

It is clearly much easier to make callous use of others from the safety of an ideological bunker. To focus past particularity and individual uniqueness to some conceptual absolute makes the marginalising and even brutalising of actual people an almost casual business. To speak in terms of *humanity* or *society*, or that well-known justification for sanctioned excess *national security*, is often preparatory to an attack on individual liberty and difference. As we suggested in Chapter Two, the ability to feel as others feel, to empathise, is a significant heroic power, it motives and drives the hero to confront the source of another's pain because it is a shared pain, there is an immediacy of experience that causes the hero to weep with the other to share their anger and outrage at villainous abuse.

In Philip Pullman's *His Dark Materials* trilogy one of the central characters, Lord Asriel, requires the release of a large amount of energy in order to open a portal to another world. His daughter, the hero of the series, Lyra, finally comes to the shocking realisation as to how he proposes to generate this energy:

> She had got out of bed, and was reaching for her clothes, and then she suddenly collapsed, and a fierce cry of despair enveloped her. She was uttering it, but it was bigger than she was; it felt as if the despair were uttering her. For she remembered his words: the energy that links body and demon *[the equivalent to the soul in Pullman's trilogy]* is immensely powerful; and to bridge the gap between worlds needed a phenomenal burst of energy...
>
> She had realised what she had done.
>
> She had struggled all this way to bring something to Lord Asriel, thinking she knew what he wanted; and it wasn't the alethiometer at all. What he wanted was a child. She had brought him Roger.
>
> That's why he'd cried out, 'I did not send for you!' when he saw her; he had sent for a child, and the fates had brought him his own daughter. Or so he'd thought, until she'd stepped aside and shown him Roger.[29]

For Asriel, dealing simply with *a child* gives him the power to dispose of that child without compunction in the service of a greater plan, having to deal with his own daughter is a different thing altogether. People who talk about the big picture often do so as a way of justifying morally dubious acts involving the lives of individual human beings. To lose one's ability to empathise is indeed a power of sorts, to act without remorse does liberate us from constraints in a terrifying way. The character of Mr Hyde from Robert Louis Stevenson's *The Strange Case of Dr. Jekyll and Mr. Hyde* is a good example of this. Jekyll's formula was not designed to turn him into a monster as such but to release him from his conscience:

There was something strange in my sensations, something indescribably new and, from its very novelty, incredibly sweet. I felt younger, lighter, happier in body; within I was conscious of a heady recklessness, a current of disordered sensual images running like a millrace in my fancy, a solution of the bonds of obligation, an unknown but not an innocent freedom of the soul. I knew myself, at the first breath of this new life, to be more wicked, tenfold more wicked, sold a slave to my original evil; and the thought, in that moment, braced and delighted me like wine.

Henry Jekyll stood at times aghast before the acts of Edward Hyde; but the situation was apart from ordinary laws, and insidiously relaxed the grasp of conscience. It was Hyde, after all, and Hyde alone, that was guilty. Jekyll was no worse; he woke again to his good qualities seemingly unimpaired; he would even make haste, where it was possible, to undo the evil done by Hyde. And thus his conscience slumbered.[30]

The villain is often construed as the one for whom nothing is beyond the pale, nothing is prohibited, no means to any end denied. Against such a foe the hero, who by definition, is limited, constrained by an ethic, is often seen to be at a disadvantage. The classic villainous strategy is the taking of hostages, the deliberate and callous use of innocent individuals in order to impose one's will upon an otherwise powerful opponent. It is for this reason that many comic book super heroes adopt a secret identity for no matter how powerful they may be, they are always vulnerable to attacks against their loved ones. While the hero knows that the villain will stop at nothing, the villain equally knows that the hero will generally become incapacitated in the face of an innocent hostage. In the real world, the harsh reality is that most governments have a 'non-capitulation to terrorists' policy on the not unreasonable grounds that once you demonstrate that vulnerability it will continually be exploited. The hero, in the main, refuses to see a distinction between one life and many lives. In the science fiction series *Babylon 5* the main heroic characters are put to the test, to see if they are truly worthy. As one is being tortured near to death the other – who has also suffered at the hands of the so-called Inquisitor – calls a halt:

> DELENN: Stop! … if you want to take someone then take me!
>
> SEBASTIAN: You would trade your life for his? I thought you had a destiny? Is that destiny not worth one life?
>
> DELENN: If I fall another will take my place and another and another!
>
> SEBASTIAN: But what of your great cause?
>
> DELENN: This is my cause! Life! One life or a billion, it's all the same!
>
> SEBASTIAN: Then you make this sacrifice willingly?
>
> DELENN: Yes.
>
> SEBASTIAN: No fame? No armies or banners or cities to celebrate your name? You will die alone and un-remarked and forgotten.[31]

While this may appear a rather simplistic analysis it once again cuts to the heart of the essential distinction between the hero and the villain – the hero makes themselves available to the other while the villain merely makes use of the other as a resource. The power of the hero, in this regard, resides in their ability to stand in the way of evil, to make of themselves a tool to confront it. The power of the villain, on the other hand, is often bound up with their ability to manipulate others, to use them as weapons.

Knowledge is power

Of course power need not be understood simply in terms of force. For hero and villain alike, the acquisition of knowledge and its effective deployment are some of the most devastating tools at their disposal:

> This is Jack Hawksmoor speaking on behalf of the Authority … our former leader, the late Jenny Sparks, was reincarnated in Singapore as a creature of near-unimaginable power. The Authority wants to use that power to build a better world. Those who oppose us do not. It is our belief that a faction within the United States military has kidnapped this child and plans to use her to destroy us. We do not recommend this course of action. Either someone tell us where Jenny

Quantum is being held or we broadcast the phone-book of every hooker in Washington.[32]

Francis Bacon's justly famous observation that *knowledge is power* has never been more relevant than it is today. While Bacon had in mind knowledge of the natural world providing us with increased technological mastery over our environment, the free flow of information via the internet has made it possible to deploy considerable economic, political and social power from the relatively safe confines of our homes and offices.

What we know and understand about the workings of the world and the people who inhabit it provides us with ability to control, to manipulate and to coerce as well as to enlighten and liberate. We all possess knowledge, at sometime or another, that can be both damaging and hurtful as well as constructive and compassionate. The key issue with respect to our themes of the heroic and the villainous is how we choose to deploy such knowledge. Knowing some embarrassing secret given to us in confidence by a friend gives us power over that friend. To repeat this information to others, either on a one to one basis or publicly via an internet posting, would cause our friend pain and anguish. To have knowledge of a person's fears and anxieties grants us the potential to exploit them for our own benefit. Blackmailers throughout history have recognised and exploited this common-place observation as indeed have advertisers and brainwashers. In order to manipulate people into submission it is important to know what makes them tick, what they want, what they fear, what values they hold. With this knowledge it has proved possible to condition whole cultures to accept war and inhuman behaviour, as well as to direct individuals towards aberrant behaviour and mindless consumption.

Knowledge, in and of itself, can be regarded as value neutral – even the knowledge of how to make a nuclear weapon could be said to be harmless scientific information until utilised in a specific way, although I realise that this is a debatable point. How we use the knowledge we have is central to our ethical stance towards the other – be they other people or the non-human world in general. Knowing that we can do a thing and actually doing it are two very different things as our utilisation of various technologies has shown us. That we have the knowledge to exploit the Earth's mineral wealth should not provide us with *carte blanche* to do so when and where we will. Similarly, knowing that our grandmothers new hat looks like a bowl of overripe fruit may be one thing, telling her this when she asks our opinion is quite another. The rather glib suggestion that knowledge and truth should always be pursued is one that, I believe, ought to be reconsidered. Hearing the truth is not always the most helpful nor even the most humane course of action and there is, I would venture, some knowledge that perhaps we ought not to possess.

The heroic character is as often as not cast in the role of an enlightening character, one who possesses either a specific body of information or general insight into the nature of the world which is used in some way to liberate others from ignorance and oppression.

In *The Matrix* trilogy of films the hero, Neo, is taught to see both the world as it truly is and the nature of the illusion pulled down over people's eyes preventing them from perceiving the real world. His mission subsequently becomes one of enlightenment, revealing the truth to those who have yet to recognise it and dismantling the false images that are designed to keep people quiescent.

> MORPHEUS: Do you believe in fate, Neo?
>
> NEO: No.
>
> MORPHEUS: Why?
>
> Neo: Because I don't like the idea that I'm not in control of my own life.
>
> MORPHEUS: I know … exactly … what you mean. Let me tell you why you're here. You're here because you know something. What you know, you can't explain. But you feel it. You've felt it your entire life. That there's something … wrong … with the world. You don't know what it is, but it's there … like a splinter in your mind, driving you mad. It is this feeling that has brought you to me. Do you … know…what I'm talking about?
>
> NEO: The Matrix?
>
> MORPHEUS: Do you want to know… what … it … is … ? The Matrix is everywhere. It's all around us, even in this very

room. You can see it when you look out your window or when you turn on your television. You can feel it when you go to work, or go to church or pay your taxes. The Matrix is the world that has been pulled over your eyes, to blind you from the truth.

NEO: What truth?

MORPHEUS: That you are a slave, Neo. Like everyone else, you were born into bondage, born into a prison that you cannot smell or taste or touch. A prison … for your mind … Unfortunately, no one can be … told … what the Matrix is … you have to see it for yourself.

(Morpheus opens a container which holds two pills: a blue one, and a red one. He puts one in each hand, and holds them out to Neo.)

MORPHEUS: This is your … last chance. After this, there is no turning back. …You take the blue pill, the story ends. You wake up and believe … whatever you want to believe. You take the red pill … you stay in wonderland … and I show you just how deep the rabbit hole goes. Remember … all I'm offering you is the truth: nothing more.[33]

Heroic and messianic figures throughout the world's history and literature have tried to give us this message, that the world we think we see is not in fact the real world or, at the very least, that it is not being properly interpreted. As we saw in Chapter One the Greek philosopher Plato famously argued that the world we perceive is nothing more than a shadow, a pale reflection of true reality that is only really available to the minds of the philosophically enlightened.

Liberation from ignorance along with a general reverence for the truth has always been part of the heroic agenda. Whether we are talking about religious heroes such as Moses, Gautama Buddha, Jesus or Mohammed, socio-political heroes of the order of Karl Marx or Martin Luther King or fantasy heroes in the mould of Gandalf, Sherlock Holmes, Batman or Dumbledore, the concern to go beyond mere appearances is the same. To see the world as it really is, to look at it with eyes that see what others miss, to even look at the world as it perhaps ought to be, is the unique capacity of the hero. Of course, the hero's superior insight into the nature of reality is as often as not a function of their having access to information and experience that goes beyond the norm. Religious heroes are portrayed as possessing transcendental insight into the nature of the world and the human condition – an insight that it is seldom possible to pass on as such but which they may encourage people to acquire for themselves. When speaking of the Buddha, for example, Joseph Campbell observes that:

> The point is that Buddhahood, Enlightenment, cannot be communicated, but only the way to Enlightenment. This doctrine of the incommunicability of the Truth which is beyond names and forms is basic to the great Oriental, as well as to the Platonic, traditions. Whereas the truths of science are communicable, being demonstrable hypotheses rationally founded on observable facts, ritual, mythology, and metaphysics are but guides to the brink of a transcendent illumination, the final step to which must be taken by each in his own silent experience.[34]

In the *Harry Potter* series of books and films the character of Dumbledore is seen in something of this light, as one who clearly knows a great deal about Harry and his destiny but allows him to find these things out for himself under a watchful eye. As we noted earlier, knowledge can be used to coerce, manipulate and control as a dominating power. By guiding to enlightenment the hero divests themselves of their privileged status as possessors of secret knowledge and equips others to see the truth for themselves. This is the epistemological equivalent to the old saying 'give a man a fish and you'll feed him for a day, teach him how to fish and he'll be able to feed himself and his family for ever'. Indeed, the same issues of power and control are operational in both instances. Providing piecemeal either information or resources places the power firmly in the hands of those who control the distribution of these things. Multinationals, government agencies and the intelligence community, for example, are all highly adept at encouraging dependency by way of a strict control over the distribution of the resources at their command. It seems to me that this is not in keeping with the heroic deployment of knowledge and power.

One of the most well-known of contemporary heroic figures – at least in the UK – is that of the Time Lord 'the Doctor' in *Doctor Who*. This time and space travelling alien figure seems to me to embody the heroic attitude towards and utilisation of the knowledge-as-power principle. The Doctor is a transcendental figure, practically immortal, free from the constraints of space and time and with the almost divine power of Gallifreian super-science at his disposal. In most cases The Doctor does not resort to brute strength or physical power in his fight against evil and villainy, more often than not it is his ability to point beyond so called 'primitive' or erroneous interpretations of reality that constitutes his acts of salvation.

> DOCTOR: That gesture you did.
> (*Primitive tribal warrior does sequence of gestures across neck and chest*)
> DOCTOR: Yes, that's the one. It's presumably to ward off evil. It's interesting because it's also the sequence for checking the seals on a 'Starfall 7' space suit. And what makes that particularly interesting is that you don't know what a 'Starfall 7' space suit is.[35]

By virtue of his transcendental, outsider status coupled with his intellectual ability the Doctor is able to see those things which are often invisible to those too close to the situation. Injustice and oppression perpetrated out of ignorance, institutionalised by way of a slavish adherence to poorly understood traditions and enforced by misappropriated power – these are the villainies that the Doctor sets himself against. In many respects this heroic mode of behaviour is something that we all experience when confronting another person with an insight into their own lives. While it is seldom a very pleasant experience, the observations of another on lives that we are far too involved in to see clearly is often very revealing. We pay the counselling and psychoanalytic professions considerable sums of money to provide this very service for us. However, it is the confronting of another out of love and compassion and genuine human empathy that renders this act an heroic one. Being prepared to suffer the animosity of a friend or loved one by calling into question their lifestyle choices, or questioning their view of reality, is, it seems to me, a truly heroic act. As we saw earlier with reference to Plato's analogy of the cave, nobody likes to be told that they have been living a lie or that their lives are in some way dysfunctional. Plato predicted that whoever risked bringing such knowledge to people would be in danger of a violent response – the life of the man Jesus, for example, proved the point.

Marxist theorists have, ever since Marx himself, placed great emphasis upon the need for consciousness raising, for increasing people's awareness of their situation. The first step in any process of liberation is making people realise that they actually need to be liberated, that they are in some way, living under oppression.

The Brazilian educator Paulo Freire famously made use of the term conscientization in his book *Pedagogy of the Oppressed*[36] to describe the learning process whereby the oppressed come to recognise both the nature of their oppression and the most effective means to transform oppressive social structures through practical action or praxis.

> The starting point for organizing the program content of education or political action must be the present, existential, concrete situation, reflecting the aspirations of the people. Utilizing certain basic contradictions, we must pose this existential, concrete, present situation to the people as a problem which challenges them and requires a response – not just at the intellectual level, but at the level of action.
>
> We must never merely discourse on the present situation, must never provide the people with programs which have little or nothing to do with their own preoccupations, doubts, hopes, and fears – programs which at times in fact increase the fears of the oppressed consciousness. It is not our role to speak to the people about our own view of the world, nor to attempt to impose that view on them, but rather to dialogue with the people about their view and ours. We must realize that their view of the world, manifested variously in their action, reflects their situation in the world. Educational and political action which is not critically aware of this situation runs the risk either of 'banking' or of preaching in the desert.[37]

Attempting to help people who do not want to be helped or, perhaps worse, do not even recognise that they need help, is a serious business indeed. While we may, as has been discussed earlier, weep at the self-destructive lifestyles of others, we may also have to ask ourselves by what right we might take a pro-active role in their unwilling salvation? Is the hero ever authorised to exercise coercive power – however benevolently intended – against the will of another or is this the equivalent of using Sauron's ring?

There are interesting parallels here with St Augustine's attitude towards heresy during the early fifth century AD. While to begin with Augustine was content to take a liberal stance on the treatment of heretics, by the time of the Donatist controversy he was taking a much more coercive position – citing Jesus' over-turning of the tables of the money changers and the parable of the wedding banquet, where guests are 'compelled' to attend, as an example of the justified use of force:

> Let the heretic be drawn from the hedges, be extracted from the thorns. Stuck in hedges, they do not want to be com-pelled: 'We will enter when we want to.' But that is not the Lord's command. He said, 'Compel them to come in.' Use compulsion outside, so freedom can arise once they are inside. (Sermon 112.8)[38]

Can we ever really compel to freedom? While we might justifiably take this rather parental stance towards children – enforcing school attendance and the eating of green vegetables against their will and for their greater good – does even the hero have a mandate to impose their will on an individual or a society or another culture? In certain instances a friend or group of friends might take it upon themselves to 'intervene' in another's life to help them confront a self-destructive addiction such as drug or alcohol dependency and this may be regarded as a courageous and compassionate act. However, when a coalition of mainly American and British forces 'intervened' in the affairs of the people of Iraq in 2003 are we talking about a similarly heroic act justifiable in the way that the previously referred to inter-vention might be? Attempting to convince an individual, or even a whole culture, that they are on a self-harming and ultimately destructive course is one thing, to actively restrain them by use of overwhelming force when they fail to take the point is quite another.

Occupancy of the so-called 'moral high ground' is, in my view, a dangerous business even if it is a business that we are forced to undertake once in while. The tendency of Western democracies to assume that 'god is on their side' is fraught with peril and the very real potential for cultural imperialism. As countries such as the United States of America and Great Britain assign themselves the role of the world's police force and the custodians of liberty and freedom – this in part as a result of their roles in the Second World War – it becomes easy for their cultures as a whole to cast themselves in the role of the hero, the one who has an almost transcendental, and indeed parental, perspective and responsibility for the rest of the world. In this respect the character of Superman, clothed in the red white and blue, could well be seen as an expression of the American psyche.

Over the years organisations such as the United Nations have sought both to debate and educate towards freedom and liberty. In some cases, however, this course of action has proved ineffective as those wielding power in particular countries continue to manoeuvre so as to maintain their power base at the expenses of the liberty and dignity of its general population. It is at this point that a range of economic and even military sanctions are brought into play. And yet, where do we derive the value systems that permit us to make ethical judgments on matters of human rights violations for example?

Establishing what in fact constitutes human nature and identity is a staggeringly difficult task that has consumed the resources of thinkers throughout human history. Do we possess an essence? A soul or spirit which has unique, perhaps even god-given value and which represents the core of what we are? Might this essence be damaged or compromised in some way such that our fundamental humanity might be put at risk? We commonly speak of inhuman behaviour and crimes against humanity and infringements of human rights, and yet without some clear notion of what we are as human beings these terms would appear to lose a great deal of their force. Think for a moment about just how difficult it is to define oneself without remainder, ask yourself 'Who and what am I?' and you will soon encounter a very large question mark. To then go on and pose the question 'What is it that could be taken from me or done to me that might jeopardise my humanity?' simply increases the size of the question mark.

Part of the attraction of the hero is their apparently clear and distinct outlook on what constitutes normality for humanity. It is this that allows them to wield their power with absolute conviction undisturbed by doubt. This is why a great many films, novels, comics and computer games portray the villains as absolutely and irredeemably evil. Daleks, Zombies, Demons, Nazis, Orcs and alien invaders (non-humanoid ones in particular) are unequivocally 'the bad guys' and as an audience we want to see them defeated by the hero, often with extreme prejudice. Unfortunately, in real life who are the good guys and who are the bad guys is seldom that clear cut. In Kevin Smith's classic 1994 cult film *Clerks* the two main characters are having a conversation about *Star Wars* which puts this particular issue into perspective:

RANDAL: So they build another Death Star, right? Now the first one they built was completed and fully operational before the Rebels destroyed it.

DANTE: Luke blew it up. Give credit where it's due.

RANDAL: And the second one was still being built when they blew it up.

DANTE: Compliments of Lando Calrissian.

RANDAL: Something just never sat right with me the second time they destroyed it. I could never put my finger on it – something just wasn't right.

DANTE: And you figured it out?

RANDAL: Well, the thing is, the first Death Star was manned by the Imperial army – storm troopers, dignitaries – the only people onboard were Imperials.

DANTE: Basically.

RANDAL: So when they blew it up, no prob. Evil is punished.

DANTE: And the second time around …?

RANDAL: The second time around, it wasn't even finished

yet. They were still under construction.

DANTE: So?

RANDAL: A construction job of that magnitude would require a helluva lot more manpower than the Imperial army had to offer. I'll bet there were independent contractors working on that thing: plumbers, aluminum siders, roofers.

DANTE: Not just Imperials, is what you're getting at.

RANDAL: Exactly. In order to get it built quickly and quietly they'd hire anybody who could do the job. Do you think the average storm trooper knows how to install a toilet main? All they know is killing and white uniforms.

DANTE: All right, so even if independent contractors are working on the Death Star, why are you uneasy with its destruction?

RANDAL: All those innocent contractors hired to do a job were killed – casualties of a war they had nothing to do with. (*notices Dante's confusion*) All right, look – you're a roofer, and some juicy government contract comes your way; you got the wife and kids and the two-storey in suburbia – this is a government contract, which means all sorts of benefits. All of a sudden these left-wing militants blast you with lasers and wipe out everyone within a three-mile radius. You didn't ask for that. You have no personal politics. You're just trying to scrape out a living.[39]

The point is that the possession of power – either in the form of knowledge or physical force – is in some respects a trivial matter compared with the issue of its legitimate application. As we said at the very beginning of this chapter, each one of us can be said to possess power by virtue of our very existence, it is what we do with it, or choose not to do with it, that renders us either heroic or villainous.

4
Villains, Monsters and Evil Masterminds

While this is something we might not like to acknowledge too freely or with too much enthusiasm the image of the villain – at least at some levels – is not unattractive to us. The 'dark side of the Force' is, undoubtedly, very seductive. The person who operates according to their own rules, who refuses to conform or be limited by convention or taboo has a strength and presence that it is hard to ignore and in some ways is hard not to admire.

Freedom is something that we tend to value very highly whether it be political freedom or freedom of expression or freedom of choice, as a species we do not like to be caged or constrained. In theological circles, for example, the importance of free will and self-determination has become central to at least one explanation for the existence of sin and evil in the world. The so-called free will defence broadly argues that even God could not enforce good behaviour upon human beings without compromising their very humanity. Immanuel Kant argues that ethical judgements are the product of the free exercise of the will and that any external motivation – such as the desire for happiness or self-interest or even altruism – renders the resulting action ethically invalid. Existentialist thinkers as diverse as Søren Kierkegaard and Jean-Paul Sartre have identified the essence of authentic human existence with our ability to make free choices, to be self-determining even if those choices inevitably commit us to a certain and more limiting path.

Radical individualism, autonomy and villainy

I think it a fair observation to make that villains generally seek to be a law unto themselves. They usually have as their primary goal power over others, world domination, control of the entire universe or, in some really ambitious instances, godhood.

Without exception this seems to be the case with the wide array of James Bond villains, for example, as they plot to impose their will upon the world through scientific means, economic means, military means and even by way of the manipulation of the media. Most science fiction villains such as the Daleks and Cybermen from *Doctor Who*, the Borg from *Star Trek*, the Replicators from *Stargate*, and so on, have a single guiding intelligence, and an insatiable drive to bring the rest of the universe under the control of that intelligence. The villain is not content with the social construction of reality, with a complex world constructed out of the interplay of diverse forces and opinions, Rather, the villain seeks to simplify the world, to recast it in to a single image where the only law is the law of their own individual, autonomous will. This, of course, is part of the reason why the Nazis, for example, make such excellent stock villains for film, novel and video game even today. We shall return to this point later.

It should concern us greatly when, for example, political leaders institute foreign and domestic policy founded upon nothing more than their own will and confidence in their own intuitive values without reference to a wider community.

In an article published in *The New York Times Magazine* towards the end of 2004 Ron Suskind made some alarming observations on the policy-making processes of President George W. Bush:

> The president has demanded unquestioning faith from his followers, his staff, his senior aides and his kindred in the Republican Party. Once he makes a decision – often swiftly, based on a creed or moral position – he expects complete faith in its rightness.
>
> The disdainful smirks and grimaces that many viewers were surprised to see in the first presidential debate are familiar expressions to those in the administration or in

Congress who have simply asked the president to explain his positions. Since 9/11, those requests have grown scarce; Bush's intolerance of doubters has, if anything, increased, and few dare to question him now. A writ of infallibility – a premise beneath the powerful Bushian certainty that has, in many ways, moved mountains – is not just for public consumption: it has guided the inner life of the White House. As Whitman told me on the day in May 2003 that she announced her resignation as administrator of the Environmental Protection Agency: 'In meetings, I'd ask if there were any facts to support our case. And for that, I was accused of disloyalty!'[1]

This tendency to base policy decisions upon 'gut feelings' and the intuitions of an individual leader has, alarmingly, prompted some to apply the highly emotive term *'Führer principle'* to Bush's style of government, we shall return to this phenomenon later in this chapter.[2]

Individualism is very much a nineteenth century word. This should come as little surprise to us as it has often been observed that the philosophy of that age does little justice to the possibility of our knowledge of other selves. Indeed, when Descartes argued that the starting point for epistemological certainty was the *Cogito* – the 'I Think' – and Kant went on to develop this notion by stating that all knowledge of the world is only ever a representation for the mind, the reality of other selves became problematic. If, as Kant's Critical Philosophy maintains, we never truly engage with *the thing in itself* but rather only with an image of that thing as it is constructed by our minds, then the other, whoever and whatever that might be, becomes something that we create in a very real sense. It is precisely our individual will that establishes the world as we perceive it to be. We impose the creative, ordering capacity of our rational will – the *Cogito* – over the chaos of sense experiences and, in godlike manner, bring forth an ordered world, in our image – surely the goal of all would be tyrants and dictators?

The desire to recreate the world in one's own image is a powerful motif in the characterisation of the villain. Characters such as Saruman from *The Lord of the Rings*, Magneto from the

X-Men and the White Witch from C.S. Lewis's Narnia novels all seek to establish what might be called a new world order. Each one wishes to structure a world that is a reflection of their own individual value system, to use force to create a world that is essentially an extension of their own will.

As early on as the mid-1820s the followers of the social scientist Claude Henri de Saint-Simon were using the term *individualisme* in this way. The Saint-Simonians heavily criticised what they recognised as the Enlightenment's glorification of the individual and expressed deep concern at the atomisation of the social order which they saw as the beginnings of anarchy.

> They used 'individualisme' to refer to the pernicious and 'negative' ideas underlying the evils of the modern critical epoch, where 'disorder, atheism, individualism and egoism' they contrasted with the prospect of 'order, religion, association and devotion'. The 'philosophers of the eighteenth Century' – men such as Helvetius, with his doctrine of 'enlightened self-interest"', Locke, Reid, Condillac, Kant and the 'atheist d'Holbach, the deist Voltaire and Rousseau' – all these 'defenders of individualism' refused to 'go back to a source higher than individual conscience'. They 'considered the individual as the centre' and 'preached egoism', providing an ideological justification for the prevailing anarchy, especially in the economic and political spheres. The 'doctrine of individualism' with its two 'sad deities ... two creatures of reason – conscience and public opinion' led to 'one political result: opposition to any attempt at organisation from a centre of direction for the moral interests of mankind, to hatred of power'.[3]

Largely as a result of Saint-Simonian ideas, *individualisme* became widely used in the nineteenth century and in France, even to the present day, carries a pejorative connotation. L. Moulin points out this pejorative sense of the word when he speaks of its 'tinge of "hubris", of "demesure"' which 'does not exist in English'.[4]

In America, of course, individualism was fast becoming a national ideal. By 1839 an article had appeared in the United States Magazine and Democratic Review which extolled individualism as a positive national value. It argued that the course of civilisation ...

> is the progress of man from a state of savage individualism to that of an individualism more elevated, moral and refined ... The peculiar duty of this country has been to exemplify and embody a civilization in which the rights, freedom and mental and moral growth of individual men should be made the highest end of all social restrictions and laws.[5]

By the end of the civil war individualism had come to occupy an important place in the American vocabulary. Ralph Waldo Emerson, for example, saw the road to perfection as involving a society of self-determined individuals 'No law can be sacred to me but that of my nature. Good and bad are but names very readily transferable to that or this; the only right is what is after my constitution, the only wrong what is against it.'[6]

It was Alexis de Tocqueville (1805–1859), the aristocratic expert on America, who was to develop one of the most influential and critical understandings of individualism. For him individualism was the natural outworking of democracy,

> involving the apathetic withdrawal of individuals from public life into a private sphere and their isolation from one another, with a consequent weakening of social bonds.

De Tocqueville saw individualism as:

> a deliberate and peaceful sentiment which disposed each citizen to isolate himself from the mass of his fellows and to draw apart with his family and friends ... it originates as much in deficiencies of mind as in perversity of heart.[7]

The ultimate end of this process, beginning with the dissolution of public life, was 'pure egoism'. As far back as the early nineteenth century De Tocqueville observed a phenomenon that has only comparatively recently received systematic treatment by modern sociologists: that is, that with increasing social mobility, social continuity begins to collapse, traditions to be lost. Individuals 'become accustomed to considering themselves always in isolation, they freely imagine that their destiny is entirely in their own hands.' The curse of a democratic system, says De Tocqueville, is that it

> not only makes each man forget his forefathers, but it conceals from him his descendants and separates him from his contemporaries; it ceaselessly throws him back on himself alone and threatens finally to confine him entirely in the solitude of his own heart.[8]

Although it is clear that De Tocqueville's ulterior motive was a concern for the status of the aristocracy, his critique of individualism still stands. His observations on the end results of social mobility and the loss of tradition and corporate responsibility have been born out by history and the examinations of the social scientists. His great fear that the individual may finally be confined to 'the solitude of his own heart' indicates that the spectre of solipsism is always found to be the true spirit of individualism. Thus, unlike in both Britain and America, in mainstream French thinking for example, *individualism* signifies social, ethical and political isolation of individual persons and their dislocation from social accountability and solidarity. In his New Year's Eve broadcast of 1968 General de Gaulle used the term in its characteristic French sense when he pointed out that:

> At the same time, it is necessary that we surmount the moral malaise which – above all among us by reason of our individualism – is inherent in modern mechanical and materialistic civilisation. Otherwise, the fanatics of destruction, the doctrinaires of negation, the specialists in demagogy, will once more have a good opportunity to exploit bitterness in order to provoke agitation, while their sterility, which they have the derisory insolence to call revolution, can lead to nothing else than the dissolution of everything into nothingness, or else to the loss of everything under the grinding oppression of totalitarianism.[9]

Clearly the dissolution of social cohesion and the atomisation of community into its component parts has long been regarded as one of the most reliable tools of the villain and the tyrant. The old adage *divide and conquer* recognises the fact that it is easier to impose one's will upon a disaggregated group of individuals than it is to impose it over a group with strong social bonds. In Tolkien's *Lord of the Rings* we are told that,

> in nothing is the power of the Dark Lord more clearly shown than in the estrangement that divides all those who still oppose him.[10]

In C. S. Lewis's *The Lion, The Witch and the Wardrobe* we are told of the White Witch who has bred fear and distrust in Narnia, 'The whole wood is full of her spies. Even some of the trees are on her side'.[11] Indeed, the totalitarian oppression of Narnia under the rule of the Witch is hardly dissimilar to that found Orwell's bleaker and more adult-orientated *Nineteen Eighty-Four*. In this later novel the fear of being spied upon by neighbours and even family help to prevent social bonds from forming making it that much easier for Big Brother to impose his will upon isolated individuals. In a chilling example of the villain's drive to break down the ties that bind humanity together O'Brien has Winston, Orwell's hapless representative of the human spirit, placed in Room 101. In this place a person is confronted by his or her greatest fear – in Winston's case it is rats let loose on his face via a specially designed mask. As the cage begins to open Winston gives up his final act of rebellion against Big Brother, his emotional connection with his lover Julia:

> The mask was closing on his face. The wire brushed his cheek. And then – no, it was not relief, only hope, a tiny fragment of hope. Too late, perhaps too late. But he had suddenly understood that in the whole world there was just one person to whom he could transfer his punishment – one body that he could thrust between himself and the rats. And he was shouting frantically, over and over.
>
> 'Do it to Julia! Do it to Julia! Not to me! Julia I don't care what you do to her. Tear her face off, strip her to the bones. Not me! Julia! Not me!'

On meeting Julia again after his ordeal they confess to each other:

> 'I betrayed you,' she said baldly.
> 'I betrayed you,' he said.

'Sometimes,' she said, 'they threaten you with something – something you can't stand up to, can't even think about. And then you say, "Don't do it to me, do it to somebody else, do it to So-and-so." ... You want it to happen to the other person. You don't give a damn what they suffer. All you care about is yourself.'

'All you care about is yourself,' he echoed.

'And after that, you don't feel the same towards the other person any longer.'

No,' he said, 'you don't feel the same.'[12]

The concept of individualism denounced in France, by De Gaulle for example, was certainly not confined to that culture alone. In Germany it was taken up by the economist Friedrich List who used it in much the same manner as did the Saint-Simonians. In his major work, *The National System of Political Economy*, written in Paris, List emphasises the organic nature of society, condemning classical economics for its tendency to abstract itself from its social context. Indeed he went on to criticise its encouragement of *laissez-faire, materialismus, particularismus,* and what he saw to be more damning than all of these, *individualismus,* which he recognised as being the altar upon which the welfare of the national community was sacrificed to the quest for individual wealth.

However, given the French influence via List, the term 'individualism' did in fact have a particularly German meaning and one which contributed to the darkest moment of that country's history. *Individualitat* carried with it the notion of individual uniqueness and originality as opposed to the Enlightenment ideal which was regarded as qualitative and abstract. It was a romantic conception which shunned all sterile categories. By the 1840s the German liberal Karl Bruggemann compared the essentially negative French understanding, as found in List, with the positive German ideal which spoke of the individual as free in matters of morals and epistemology – a view that would find a more enduring and influential voice in the philosopher Nietzsche. Thus, this new German individualism had to do with uniqueness and difference as opposed to atomisation, which characterised its Enlightenment understanding.

In his essay 'The Ideas of Natural Law and Humanity in World Politics', Ernst Troeltsch drew a distinction between West-European and German thought. The former he saw as exhibiting 'an eternal, rational and divinely ordained system of Order', the latter as 'individual, living and perpetually new incarnations of an historically creative Mind'. He therefore went on to conclude that:

> Those who believe in an eternal and divine Law of Nature, the Equality of man and a sense of Unity pervading mankind, and who find the essence of Humanity in these things, cannot but regard the German doctrine as a curious mixture of mysticism and brutality.

On the other hand, those who regard history as a process which produces ever new and 'unique individualities'

> are bound to consider the West-European world of ideas as a World of cold rationalism and equalitarian atomism, a world of superficiality and Pharisaism.[13]

This Romantic conception of personal and qualitative individuality very soon developed into a form of nationalism where the uniqueness of a particular people, an individual nation or state, was brought to the fore.

This aspect of the development of individualism is crucial for two reasons. Firstly, it illustrates how mass movements or nationalistic fervour, while often appearing to take the form of community are in actual fact nothing more than a form of extended individualism. Secondly, one can already see enshrined in this attitude of qualitative individualism coupled with a heightened sense of racial uniqueness the framework around which Nazi Germany would construct itself. It is here, at the point of a nation's confidence in its cultural uniqueness and self-sufficiency, that folk sentiment meets with the intellectual ideas of its thinkers and leaders. Hitler's appropriation of Nietzsche's Superman was not, contrary to popular belief, the motivation behind his eugenics programme. Hitler was not primarily concerned with the creation of a new biological species, but rather with the creation of a new culture, an extension of the German cultural ideal. Ernst Nolte points out that

> 'To create' means for Nietzsche primarily to give 'meaning' and define values. The superman not only provides peoples and times with their tables and values: he creates 'meaning' for the earth as a whole and for all aeons to come. 'He who defines values and controls the will of millennia by controlling the most superior natures, is the super man.'[14]

Nietzsche speaks of the need to escape from what he calls the 'morality of custom', a slavish acquiescence to the status quo and standards of behaviour established and enforced by the pressure of consensus and the weight of tradition. In *The Gay Science* he writes:

> With morality the individual is led into being a function of the herd and to ascribing value to himself only as a function … Morality is the herd instinct in the individual.[15]

By contrast, the true autonomous individual is the superman, the one who establishes value for himself without reference to external influences:

> the sovereign individual, something which resembles only itself, which has broken loose again from the morality of custom – the autonomous individual beyond morality (for 'autonomous' and 'moral' are mutually exclusive terms) – in short, the human being who possesses his own independent and enduring will, who is entitled to make promises – and in him a proud consciousness, quivering in every muscle, of what has finally been achieved and given living embodiment in him: a real consciousness of power and freedom, a feeling of completion for human beings generally.[16]

Nietzsche clearly wishes to valorise the anonymous individual, and sees in it the most heroic manifestation of humanity – a humanity free to revel in self-definition and to exercise *the will to power*. This image of the Superman he places in contrast to the ideals of both Christianity and the Enlightenment which he regards as enslaving traditions that impose damaging restraints upon human freedom.

Once again we would have to say that the unlimited freedom that Nietzsche preaches is the true destiny of humanity – the end of the process linking animal to Superman – and it is not without its appeal. Freedom is, as we have said, one of our most cherished ideals and yet, it is generally recognised that for a society to function properly certain freedoms have to be sacrificed for the sake of the greater good.

Back in the seventeenth century John Locke made a similar point as he sought to develop the notion of a social contract, a socio-political tool for maintaining social cohesion in the face of the natural freedom of humanity. Locke argues that in their natural state all human beings find themselves in

> a state of perfect freedom to order their actions, and dispose of their possessions and persons as they think fit, within the bounds of the law of Nature, without asking leave or depending upon the will of any other man.
>
> A state also of equality, wherein all the power and jurisdiction is reciprocal, no one having more than another, there being nothing more evident than that creatures of the same species and rank, promiscuously born to all the same advantages of Nature, and the use of the same faculties, should also be equal one amongst another, without subordination or subjection.[17]

He goes on to argue that this natural freedom is only curtailed out of respect for the freedom of others:

> all men may be restrained from invading others' rights, and from doing hurt to one another, and the law of Nature be observed, which willeth the peace and preservation of all mankind, the execution of the law of Nature is in that state put into every man's hands, whereby every one has a right to punish the transgressors of that law to such a degree as may hinder its violation. For the law of Nature would, as all other laws that concern men in this world, be in vain if there were nobody that in the state of Nature had a power to execute that law, and thereby preserve the innocent and restrain offenders; and if any one in the state of Nature may punish another for any evil he has done, every one may do

so. For in that state of perfect equality, where naturally there is no superiority or jurisdiction of one over another, what any may do in prosecution of that law, every one must needs have a right to do.[18]

It seems to me that at the very heart of the notion of the villain is a refusal to submit to the social contract – for whatever reason – and a wilful attempt at exploiting the fact that the rest of society chooses to be bound by it. The simple fact of the matter is that, for the most part, villains do not play by the rules.

In Tim Burton's 1996 film *Mars Attacks!* the Martian villains constantly flout Earth conventions by opening fire on peace delegations, government officials attempting to negotiate and even a dove of peace released in their honour. In one scene we see a group of Martians pursuing some fleeing humans and while firing on them with their ray guns you hear them calling out 'Don't run, we are your friends!'

Much has been made of the so-called *Führer principle* as a description of the way in which all authority was vested in the person of Adolf Hitler during the dominance of National Socialism in the Germany of the 1930s and 1940s. In spite of our general perceptions of totalitarian Nazi Germany being run as a well oiled machine the truth of the matter seems rather more chaotic. The *Führer principle* related to the demand for absolute obedience to the authority of one's superior – principally Adolf Hitler himself. One's duty to the Führer superceded any other claim that might be made on one by morality, religion, tradition and even the state itself. It was perfectly possible for a person within the Nazi party to circumvent all 'official channels' by appealing directly to their Führer. It is precisely for this reason that at the Nuremberg trials so many Nazi war criminals felt it appropriate to deploy the 'we were only following orders' defence.[19]

In his book giving an account of the origins and development of Hitler's 'SS' Heinz Hohne makes this important observation:

With the advent of the Nazis the State came under the control of a Party which, though apparently monolithic, was in fact the most contradictory in the history of German party politics. Held together only by the charismatic leadership of Hitler, a peculiar collection of factions and splinter groups milled around.[20]

In 1938 Hitler informed a hundred and fifty thousand Nazi party officials in Nuremberg that they were the German people. As Nolte points out:

> the ruling elite of the Nordic race nucleus rose up in varying degrees, while this elite was in turn ruled absolutely by the Führer, whose 'will was the constitution'.[21]

For the person or culture that regards themselves as completely autonomous in matters of epistemology and ethics there are no controls save that of the individual will. The complete disaffiliation from the rest of humanity epistemically through the 'I think', ethically by way of the 'self-valuating will' and socially through a process of privatization make all things possible. Consider for a moment the future of Eastern Europe as outlined in *Hitler's Table Talk*:

> Underlying everything is the total disfranchisement of the subjugated. They have no claims of any kind, except an early death. They are forbidden to learn to read and write; to concern themselves with history or politics is a crime worthy of death. Any communication whatever going beyond the confines of the village is strictly prohibited.[22]

This point of view is summed up succinctly by one of the Doctor's Dalek adversaries: 'There is only one form of life that matters – Dalek life! Obey your orders'.[23]

Similarly, Harry Potter's arch enemy Lord Voldemort, inspires his puppet Quirrell: 'A foolish young man I was then, full of ridiculous ideas about good and evil. Lord Voldemort showed me how wrong I was. There is no good and evil, there is only power, and those too weak to seek it.'[24]

One of the most striking examples of this notion of the villain as autonomous individual motivated simply by the desire for power over others is found in the character of Davros, the creator of the Daleks. In a now classic confrontation between himself and the Doctor, the Doctor poses an ethical question intended to prompt Davros into reconsidering his design for the Daleks:

> DOCTOR: 'Davros, if you had created a virus in your labora-
> tory. Something contagious and infectious that killed on
> contact. A virus that would destroy all other forms of life
> … would you allow its use?'
>
> DAVROS: 'It is an interesting conjecture.'
>
> DOCTOR: 'Would you do it?'
>
> DAVROS: 'The only living thing … the microscopic organism
> … reigning supreme … A fascinating idea.'
>
> DOCTOR: 'But would you do it?'
>
> DAVROS: 'Yes. Yes. To hold in my hand, a capsule that con-
> tained such power. To know that life and death on such a
> scale was my choice. To know that the tiny pressure on my
> thumb, enough to break the glass, would end everything.
> Yes. I would do it. That power would set me up above the
> gods. And through the Daleks I shall have that power!'[25]

William Shakespeare was also well aware of the villainous capacities of the individual who saw themselves as in some qualitative way separate from the rest of humanity. In the character of Macbeth we see a man, a loyal hero of the crown, quickly descend into radical egoism fuelled by the promise of achievement, personal glory and invulnerability. The play seems to rotate around the notion of the unnatural and the monstrous, the inversion of values; the opening act introduces this theme when the three witches are heard to chant 'Fair is foul and foul is fair'. By Act Four we have Macbeth consenting to any atrocity if it will secure him the information necessary for his continued advancement:

> I conjure you, by that which you profess,
> Howe'er you come to know it, answer me:
> Though you untie the winds and let them fight
> Against the churches; though the yesty waves
> Confound and swallow navigation up;
> Though bladed corn be lodged and trees blown down;
> Though castles topple on their warders' heads;
> Though palaces and pyramids do slope
> Their heads to their foundations; though the treasure

Of nature's germens tumble all together,
Even till destruction sicken; answer me
To what I ask you.[26]

However, the ultimate dislocation of Macbeth from his humanity has not yet come, it is only when he has received the assurance that 'none of woman born shall harm Macbeth' is he free from the final constraint, fear of reprisal. No longer having to concern himself with personal safety Macbeth is free to indulge in any whim or bloody deed, as we see when he has Macduff's family slaughtered. In Roman Polanski's 1971 film version of the play the final Act brings out all the confidence and autonomous disdain for lesser men that Macbeth clearly feels as he strides among his enemies proclaiming

… swords I smile at, weapons laugh to scorn,
Brandish'd by man that is of woman born.

His invulnerability, real or imagined, places him beyond account-ability or harm, he is the Superman. Only when the charm is broken is he finally destroyed.

It would seem that while we must certainly acknowledge the importance of individual identity over those who would see it subsumed within a greater whole – the state or a mob or some other amorphous collective – the danger of overstating individu-ality must not be overlooked. To define ourselves in isolation from others, to see our humanity as residing purely and simply in our autonomous self somehow disconnected from the rest of the world is, in my view, a dangerous thing. History has shown us that villainous and inhuman acts are considerably easier to justify when a person, culture or race understands itself as being unrelated to the rest of humanity. This is surely the message contained within the Hebrew traditional story about the first murderer, Cain, who upon being confronted by God concerning the death of his brother Able replied 'Am I my brother's keeper?' Enlightenment resourced western culture has, as we have outlined above, tended to operate with a reductionist view of human being as isolated individual: the 'I' found in Descartes 'I think therefore I am'. With this in mind we in the West need to be particularly aware of our tendency towards isolation.[27]

The beast within

It has become something of a commonplace, certainly post Freud, to suggest that the evil that we do issues not out of any rational or conscious desire to do wrong, but rather is the expression of some hidden 'beast within', a lawless predatory creature that wills to do all the reckless wickedness that civilization, society, religion and ethics are designed to keep submerged and suppressed.

The nineteenth century anthropologist and criminologist Cesare Lombroso, for example, argued that criminals were a throwback to a less evolved and thus more primitive humanity. Such individuals, he maintained, manifested a range of 'brutish' characteristics which involved a low forehead, large jaws and a tendency to stoop and thus appear smaller. Hence the use of the term 'upright' to indicate both moral and physical superiority.[28] We can see this clearly in H. G. Wells's portrayal of the brutish Morlocks in his famous science fiction novel *The Time Machine*.

Classically the notion of 'the beast' carries with it a sense of the feral, the untamed and the dangerous. One of the best examples of this in literature is Robert Louis Stevenson's *The Strange Case of Dr Jekyll and Mr Hyde* where saintly and repressed Victorian medic Dr Jekyll discovers a formula which transforms him into his bestial dark side Mr Hyde, a brutal self-indulgent man completely outside conventional ethics and civilization.[29]

The Marvel comic character *The Incredible Hulk*, created in 1962, explores similar ground. Although the Hulk is, for the most part, never portrayed as a villain but rather as a misunderstood and persecuted creature – in the style of Frankenstein's creation – writer Stan Lee clearly borrows from the Jekyll and Hyde story as well. The notion of the physically unassuming and morally upright scientist Bruce Banner being transformed by gamma radiation into a physically powerful but intellectually challenged beast is a close parallel to Stevenson's story.

As is so often the case with persistent western cultural perspectives classical Greek thought can be seen as playing a significant role in the development of the ideas and themes associated with beastliness. One of the principle questions that concerned Greek thinkers and writers and continues to concern us now is 'Why do I do bad things?' which of course easily gets recast as 'Who can I blame for my bad behaviour?'

For early, pre-Platonic, Greek thinkers the answer was easy – the gods are responsible. For the most part the gods were regarded as a fickle bunch who interfered in the lives and indeed the psyches of humanity at the drop of a hat. It was perfectly acceptable to argue therefore that aberrant behaviour was not actually our responsibility and that we were being manipulated by higher powers, in other words – the devil made me do it! This is a very strong motif in *The Lord of the Rings*, for example, where both Sauron, Saruman and the Ring itself are seen as exerting a powerful seductive force over the minds of even the most noble of heroes such as Boromir.

> 'I am a true man, neither thief or tracker. I need your Ring: that you know now; but I give you my word that I do not desire to keep it ... You can say I was too strong and took it by force. For I am too strong for you, Halfling,' he cried; and suddenly he sprang over the stone and leaped at Frodo. His fair and pleasant face was hideously changed; a raging fire was in his eyes.[30]

This attitude was not limited to the Greeks, in the Hebrew scriptures the earliest example of 'trying to get off the hook' can be found when God confronts Adam and Eve with their wrong-doing and asks for an explanation – Adam blames Eve and indirectly God and then Eve blames the Serpent who is both a beast and a supernatural figure:

> The Man said 'The woman you put here with me – she gave me some fruit from the tree and I ate it' ... The woman said 'The serpent deceived me, and I ate.[31]

However, as the gods became more noble and less malicious, largely as the result of their rehabilitation through Plato, a new scapegoat had to be found – the so-called 'beast within'.

Plato argues that the human being, as essentially a rational soul, can be subverted by the physical world, the world of matter, the world of the animal. This is a recurring theme throughout western thinking, that a tension exists between humanity as spirit/consciousness and humanity as mere animal flesh. The spirit – the true seat of human identity – is governed by rational principles and the rule of the will while the flesh is dominated by its lusts and passions.

It is telling that whenever Plato talks about evil then animal imagery is not far away. What he has in mind is not any particular animal but a monstrous hybrid that stalks us and seeks to subvert the pure rationality of our soul.[32] The beasts that lurk within us, says Plato:

> bestir themselves in dreams, when the gentler part of the soul slumbers, and the control of Reason is withdrawn. Then the wild Beast in us, full-fed with meat and drink, becomes rampant and shakes off sleep to go in quest of what will gratify its own instincts. As you know, it will cast off all shame and prudence at such moments and stick at nothing. In phantasy it will not shrink from intercourse with mother or anyone else. Man, god or brute, or from forbidden food or any deed of blood. It will go to any lengths of shamelessness and folly.[33]

This rather bleak perspective on human nature, whether out of fear or the desire for control over the masses, has been extraordinarily influential throughout Western cultural history. The notion that only reason, backed-up by the human will, prevents the beast from surfacing can be found in a variety of places.

The early Christian tradition via Augustine borrows heavily from Plato and so we should not be surprised to find this attitude to human 'beastliness' echoed in his work. Even though Augustine does not denigrate the physical as Plato does he certainly sees it as subordinate to the spiritual. The transmission of original sin from one generation to the next is understood by Augustine to take place during the sex act when reason is off its guard. Human wickedness, maintains Augustine, issues out of the wrong prioritising of flesh over spirit.

Later in the eighteenth century the philosopher Immanuel Kant made a similar point when he argued that 'Sexuality exposes man to the danger of equality with the beasts'.[34]

In fact this is the corner stone of Kantian ethics, that we are creatures of animal instinct and rational will and it is only the exercise of will which prevents our flesh from dominating us, it is only the capacity for 'will' that renders us capable of doing our duty. This is a view that we find occurring throughout the nineteenth century in philosophers and theologians alike. Nineteenth century liberal theologians such as Ritschl and Harnack put great emphasis upon the will as the source of ethical motivation and thus spirituality.

For Albrecht Ritschl (1822–1889) The whole point of religion was not to provide us with knowledge of god – directly or indirectly – but to overcome the dualism at the heart of human existence. The human being is a being in contradiction, a divided being that exists both as *animal* – part of the natural world – and *spiritual* – a personal being possessing a will. It is the will which permits us to overcome our animal nature and to achieve a specific destiny. This is the example of Christ.

Of course the notion of the will as something that might free us from the lawless animal side of our nature is seen in a somewhat different way in the work of Nietzsche who argues that it is precisely the will which frees the lawless animal within:

> What is the great dragon which the spirit is no longer inclined to call Lord and God? 'Thou-Shalt' is the great dragon called. But the spirit of the Lion saith, 'I will' ...
>
> My brethren, wherefore is there need of the Lion in the spirit? Why sufficeth not the beast of burden, which renounceth and is reverent?
>
> To create new values – that even the lion cannot yet accomplish but to create itself freedom, for new creating – that can the might of the lion do.
>
> To create itself freedom, and give a holy Nay even unto duty: for that, my brethren, there is need of the lion.[35]

The animal image is seen here as the free spirit, a being of strength that can break free of convention and traditional morality and value. The reference to duty at the end of the last quote is a clear attack on the Kantian categorical imperative. Thus, the beast in Nietzsche is something to embrace, providing us with liberating power, while in Plato and others it is something to be feared as it compromises and undermines the rationally informed will.

Fairy tales such as *Little Red Riding Hood*, and tales of werewolves in general have, as their subtext, the notion of an uncontrolled inner demon which can only be contained by reason, the will and convention. Often the notion of the sub-merged 'beast' is associated with sexual excess and rapacious-ness. There are no werewolf films that I am aware of that don't ooze sexual tension from every pore![36]

In the classic 1941 film *The Wolf Man* we encounter the rational engineer Larry Talbot transformed into a rapacious, murdering beast against his will and to his deep distress. Larry is portrayed as a victim, as someone to be pitied because the evil he committed was not his responsibility. As the Gypsy wise woman Maleva notes in the poem that has become synonymous with this film:

> Even a man who's pure in heart and says his prayers by night may become a wolf when the wolfbane blooms and the autumn moon is bright.

However, while the idea of our animal side has become a convenient scapegoat for all our most basic thoughts and desires, it has been strongly argued by the likes of Mary Midgley and others that this point of view is unhelpful and inaccurate both with regard to humanity and animals. It seems demonstrably the case that animals are by no means 'beastly'. Wolves in particular are clearly very social creatures. Midgley points out that far from being sexually promiscuous and rapacious most animals have rather limited sexual appetites as they have a 'mating season'. It is human beings who are obsessed with the sex act.

It has long been recognised that humanity is one of the very few species that prays on itself and makes war – certainly on the scale that we do and with our endless inventiveness. Animals, far from being lawless chaotic creatures such as Mr Hyde, seem to be creatures of order and society.

Thus it would seem that Freud's Id, the lawless subconscious, may very well be all ours. We cannot take comfort in a cosy dualism which sets our pure real, spiritual self off against the alien animal which is somehow not us but some primal force seeking to subvert us. If we cannot say 'the devil made me do it', and we cannot blame some beast within over which we have no control, then who or what do we blame? Are we only ever as good as the laws and conventions that constrain us? Do we merely fear getting caught? What villainy are we as human beings – body and soul – capable of and why?

For the most part I think we would like to believe that the evil beast-like aspect of our character is nothing more than an aberration, a left over remnant of a more primitive stage in our development. The whole language of 'beastliness' rests, in part, on this belief. The notion that there is an equal sided struggle taking place for our soul – as we see with Jekyll and Hyde – and that either aspect might gain dominance at a moment's notice is not one we would happily entertain. The prevailing belief, it would seem, is that it is the civilized, rational side of our character that is in control, that is dominant.

This conflict between the light and the dark side is made particularly prominent in the *Star Wars* series of films. In *The Return of the Jedi* (1982) Luke confronts the evil Emperor who has already corrupted his father transforming him from the Jedi knight Anakin Skywalker into Sith lord Darth Vader. The Emperor sees the struggle going on inside Luke:

> You want this, don't you? *(gestures to Luke's lightsaber)* The hate is swelling in you now. Take your Jedi weapon. Use it. I am unarmed. Strike me down with it. Give in to your anger. With each passing moment, you make yourself more my servant.

In the classic 1956 science fiction film *Forbidden Planet*, the invisible monster that goes on a savage killing spree is finally identified as the primitive unconscious of the man of science Professor Morbius. While awake Morbius is a rational man of peace who appears to be able to keep his temper in check. However, as soon as Morbius sleeps his subconscious 'beast within', empowered by an ancient alien device, is set loose to do all those things that the conscious Morbius perhaps only ever dreamt of in his darkest nightmares. It is at this point that

Morbius finally understands what it was that killed off the enlightened civilization of the Krell thousands of years earlier:

> like you the Krell forgot one deadly danger. Their own subconscious hate and lust for destruction … And so those mindless beasts of the subconscious had access to a machine that could *never* be shut down. The secret devil of every soul on the planet all set free at once to loot and maim and take revenge, Morbius! And kill!

As the creature comes ever closer, breaking down all barriers before it in its desire to punish Morbius's daughter for abandoning him for the young starship captain Adams, the professor cries out in anguish:

> My evil self is at that door and I have no power to stop him!

I wonder how many times we have thought precisely that? That we are in the grip of something that we cannot control and that is intent upon doing us and other harm?

In many ways Western civilization has had this belief in the need to control the wild and the primitive at its very core: In its colonial policies – we feel we have the right and duty to police more 'primitive' cultures – in its attitude to child rearing – children are understood as undeveloped primitive creatures of instinct and ego, particularly so in Victorian times – and in our attitude to animals – particularly as witnessed in the phenomenon of the Zoo where animals are chained and caged.

Primitive savage beasts must be and indeed can be controlled by the exercise of will and reason. When the beast does emerge it is generally seen as slipping free during a weak moment, as with Professor Morbius, when reason is no longer fully in charge.

Francisco Goya's famous late eighteenth-century etching *The Sleep of Reason Produces Monsters* can be seen as reflecting this notion, that only conscious reason holds back the demons and monsters that lurk within the heart of humanity.[37]

In the Jekyll and Hyde story while Dr Jekyll appears to be controlling the beast, experimenting under scientific conditions and utilising a formula that was the product of his reason, eventually the bestial Hyde manages to free himself without Jekyll's aid.

Indeed, it seems to be a motif in literature and film that the beast always finds a way to escape and that it cannot be controlled, short of its destruction, once released. Classic monsters such as Dracula, Frankenstein and Mr Hyde are portrayed as being let loose upon society by well-meaning and apparently civilized individuals who consider themselves to be in some way *in control*.[38]

Bram Stoker's Count Dracula[39] is, effectively, contained within the environs of his ancestral castle, prevented from travelling vast distances for fear of being unable to find a suitable resting place while in transit. It is only with the advent of sophisticated transportation, and the good offices of his lawyer Jonathan Harker, that he is able to take up residence in England and prey upon its population.

> I shuddered as I bent over to touch him, and every sense in me revolted at the contact, but I had to search, or I was lost. The coming night might see my own body a banquet in a similar way to those horrid three. I felt all over the body, but no sign could I find of the key. Then I stopped and looked at the Count. There was a mocking smile on the bloated face which seemed to drive me mad. This was the being I was helping to transfer to London, where, perhaps, for centuries to come he might, amongst its teeming millions, satiate his lust for blood, and create a new and ever-widening circle of semi-demons to batten on the helpless.[40]

Dracula clearly understands himself to be apart from and superior to the rest of humanity by virtue of his status as an aristocrat as much as by his vampiric nature. Humanity is perceived by him to be little more than cattle, livestock to be herded and consumed. Once again we encounter the villain as disengaged, autonomous, rapacious and concerned only with the power to dominate and control. Of course when the blood hunger comes upon Dracula he, along with almost every vampire that has been portrayed after him, is helpless in its grip and becomes a creature of feral instinct.

In the immensely successful Marvel series of comics and films featuring the X-Men – a band of mutant heroes feared by society because of their differences and powers – the most popular character is that of Wolverine. Known variously by his personal name, Logan, and by the codename given to him by the military, Weapon X, Wolverine could be seen as a study in self-control. While undeniably one of the good guys, Wolverine is prone to bouts of berserker rage that often results in the death of his enemies and this normally through the savage use of his own claws. How Logan manages to fight on the side of good, as a hero, while at the same time seeking to maintain control over his murderous urges is an important factor in his popularity. The Wolverine is not a 'red white and blue' hero in the style of Superman or Captain America – heroes who stop short at murder and brutality – the Wolverine, like the Batman and the Punisher, possesses a barely suppressed rage. Indeed it is this rage that paradoxically provides all of these anti-heroes with the strength to fight as well as causing them to fear what they are capable of. In a story which has Wolverine's control over his savagery compromised he enters a house in which the whole family have been butchered:

NEURI: Do not torture yourself

LOGAN: I gotta do this … for my own sanity. I've killed in battle, man to man … but this is different. I always knew the danger of berserker rages … what might happen if I completely lost control … but they made me feel it … enjoy it …

NEURI: But you did not do it …

LOGAN: But it felt like I did … can't you understand? It's in my memory, it's part of me … I'm gonna make 'em pay, gonna kill… kill … [41]

In one of the Batman's conflicts with the considerably more powerful Superman he makes this interesting observation about why, even when under the malevolent control of another, Superman will not hurt him:

If Clark wanted to, he could use his superspeed and squish me into the cement. But I know how he thinks. Even more than Kryptonite, he's got one big weakness. Deep down, Clark's essentially a good person ... and deep down. I'm not.[42]

The Christian theologian Wolfhart Pannenberg argues that what Freud called the ego, the animal or 'beast within' should actually be viewed as determinative for human existence:

all human beings are determined by the centrality of their ego. They individually experience themselves as the center of their world. Thus they experience space as in front and in back, right and left, with their vantage point at any given moment functioning as the center to which all is related. They experience time as past and future that are divided by the point which is their present, and are thus relative to them. And we experience everything else as being, like time and space, relative to our ego as to the center of our world ... It is not at all the case that egocentricity first makes its appearance in the area of moral behaviour; rather, it already determines the whole way in which we experience the world.[43]

The suggestion here is that we are – at an essential level – egocentric beasts, that this is our natural state and that it is so prior to any ethical interpretation of our behaviour. The fact that a small child might help itself to food or lash out when frustrated or make some hurtful comment to another may very well not be an expression of moral wrong doing but simply animal instinct. For the most part, as we mature, we gain increasing levels of control over our behaviour and the external expression of our inner thoughts and feelings. We do indeed seem to be able, in the main, to contain our impulses and desires and in spite of our awareness of the presence of a dark side within we seldom allow it to surface – at least not for very long. I say in the main because as we are well aware there are those who appear to give full rein to their desires and instincts in a Mr Hyde sort of way. However, it seems to me that this has more to do with the autonomous individualism we spoke of earlier than any 'beast within' forcing us to act against our will. As Joseph Conrad famously commented, 'The belief in a supernatural source of evil is not necessary; men alone are quite capable of every wickedness.'[44]

The drive towards radical individualism, so characteristic of the post-enlightenment paradigm, has the potential, I believe, to generate villainy on a grand scale. The imposition of a single worldview or value system sourced from the mind of an autonomous individual free from the checks and balances of social or communal engagement is a dangerous thing indeed. It is, by the way, the suspicion with which postmodernism regards such grand narratives that, in my view, represents the most significant achievement of the movement. Its critique of *meta-narratives*, single all encompassing world views, is a timely reminder of the multifaceted complexity of human existence and the limits of our perceptual and epistemic horizons. At a time when globalisation and talk of a new world order are common political currency it is important that we remain alert to the dangers of the totalitarian imposition of a single will upon the whole of humanity.

True villainy has to do not with our passions or instincts nor even with the dark thoughts we all have from time to time. True villainy has to do with the desire to dominate, to subsume the other within the individual self and that without compunction. The villain would appear to lack empathy, the ability to feel for others, to see themselves as part of a larger whole. The villain uses the world and the people in it from a distance, as pure resource. It is little wonder that multinational corporations, bureaucracies and political parties of all kinds are often viewed with suspicion and cast in the role of the villain as they become increasingly disengaged from ordinary human lives. Faceless corporations and other powerful organisations appear to care little for the lives of actual human beings concerning themselves rather with abstractions, apparently for the sake of greater efficiency and objectivity.

For all that we may be rightly critical of his notion of the Superman Nietzsche does have a number of useful lessons to teach us, one of the most important I believe is enshrined in this famous warning:

> Anyone who fights with monsters should make sure that he does not in the process become a monster himself. And

when you look for a long time into an abyss, the abyss also looks into you.[45]

To collapse into villainy is not to be taken over by the 'beast within' but to have our connection with others compromised. This can happen gradually, even while apparently combating other forms of villainy and evil. As we noted in a previous chapter, the utilising of the methods and tools of the enemy – methods and tools designed to manipulate and dominate – is often enough to turn us into the very monsters we seek to combat. The Batman's refusal to take a life, Gandalf's refusal to use the Ring, Luke's refusal to make use of the power of the dark side of the Force, all of these stand as examples of the heroic rejection of the power to impose one's will upon another.

In the final analysis, and this may seem rather a banal thing to say after all that has gone before, the worst thing one might have to say about villains, both real and imagined, is that with respect to other human beings and the rest of the world – they simply do not care.

5

Conclusion

When Humphrey Bogart's Rick – from the classic 1942 film *Casablanca* – chooses to give up the love of his life, Ilsa, for her future happiness, for her husband's happiness and for the good of the anti-Nazi resistance that Victor helps lead, he commits an act of heroism which, in my view, ranks alongside Luke Skywalker's blowing up of the evil Empire's Deathstar, or the Fantastic Four's defeat of the planet devouring Galactus or Sauron's defeat at the hands of Aragorn's forces. I should like to quote his famous runway speech here for two reasons. Firstly, it is an iconic moment for heroic fiction and secondly, I've been waiting my whole life for a legitimate opportunity to get it into a piece of writing:

> ILSA: You're saying this only to make me go.
>
> RICK: I'm saying it because it's true. Inside of us we both know you belong with Victor. You're part of his work, the thing that keeps him going. If that plane leaves the ground and you're not with him, you'll regret it.
>
> ILSA: No.
>
> RICK: Maybe not today, maybe not tomorrow, but soon, and for the rest of your life.
>
> ILSA: But what about us?
>
> RICK: We'll always have Paris. We didn't have, we'd lost it, until you came to Casablanca. We got it back last night.
>
> ILSA: And I said I'd never leave you.

> RICK: And you never will. But I've got a job to do, too. Where I'm going you can't follow. What I've got to do you can't be any part of. Ilsa, I'm no good at being noble, but it doesn't take much to see that the problems of three little people don't amount to a hill of beans in this crazy world. Someday you'll understand that. Now, now ... Here's looking at you, kid.[1]

Throughout this book we have encountered heroes and villains of all kinds with all manner of powers and motivations. There are those with paranormal abilities, which they choose to use for good or ill, for themselves exclusively or for others. There are those with special knowledge, insight into the world and its operations that provide them with the power to manipulate those around them to their benefit or to their harm, to liberate or to dominate. We have spoken of those whose lives have been scarred by personal tragedy and who have allowed this event to shape their future behaviour, to define them as particular kinds of heroes or villains.

To a significant, albeit simplistic, extent the hero and the villain may be seen as aspects of the same tragic character, one who encounters a crisis of some sort or another and chooses to respond in a particular way. It is in the nature of the response to circumstances *in extremis* that we see the heroic and villainous personas manifest themselves.

In Alan Moore's *Batman: The Killing Joke* this theme is explored by way of a comparison between the Batman and his arch enemy the psychotic Joker. The Joker takes it upon himself to demonstrate that the Dark Knight is as much the result of 'one bad day' as he is himself. Having escaped from Arkham Asylum the Joker targets Batman's long-time friend Police Commissioner Gordon. Having crippled his daughter and physically abused him the Joker sets out to prove that if you push anyone far enough they will become as mad and anti-social as he is. The Batman arrives at the Joker's abandoned carnival hideout and frees Gordon who, in spite of everything and far from being reduced to the psychotic condition the Joker expects, admonishes his friend to capture the Joker legitimately.

GORDON: I want him brought in by the book!

BATMAN: I'll do my best.

GORDON: By the book, you hear? We have to show him! We
have to show him that our way works![2]

The Joker, unaware of his failure to break Jim Gordon, taunts the Batman via the carnival's PA system as the Dark Knight seeks to track him down:

You see, it doesn't matter if you catch me and send me back to the asylum… Gordon's been driven mad, I've proved my point. I've demonstrated there's no difference between me and everyone else! All it takes is one bad day to reduce the sanest man alive to lunacy. That's how far the world is from where I am. Just one bad day. You had a bad day once, am I right? I know I am. I can tell. You had a bad day and everything changed. Why else would you dress up like a flying rat? You had a bad day, and it drove you as crazy as everyone else … only you won't admit it! You have to keep pretending that life makes sense, that there is some point to all this struggling! God, you make me want to puke.[3]

While the Batman informs the Joker that Gordon remains sane and that perhaps it is a flaw in the Joker's own character that made him what he is, the last half a dozen panels of the graphic novel, depicting the Batman and the Joker laughing maniacally together over a joke, serves to reinforce the notion of similarity between the two of them.

Richard Reynolds makes this point:

What makes Batman so different from Superman is that his character is formed by confronting a world which refuses to make sense. His experiences might have taught him to be wholly cynical – yet he continues to risk life and limb in a one-man war against crime. Most of his arch-enemies speak in riddles … all in their own way suggest qualities which, whilst evil or antisocial in their results, derive from a radical inability to function in the everyday world – in short, sketches of various types of madness. All Batman's most effective scripters and artists have understood that madness is a part of Batman's special identity... [4]

Perhaps the Joker's notion of 'one bad day' does indeed make sense but so then does the idea of what you do with the memory of that day. That the Batman is often portrayed as being only a hair's breadth from the dark side is a commonplace observation and one that is fairly easy to demonstrate and even to accept. Yet the point is he manages to master that tragic moment when he saw his parents gunned down on the street. While that one bad day does doubtless serve to define and motivate him it does not own or corrupt him. He refuses to become the thing he hates, a killer – as much as he might want to at times. Perhaps that is also at the heart of the heroic soul, the recognition that we are indeed potential killers and are fundamentally self-serving and anti-social but that we can choose not to give in to these character traits. As Star Trek's Captain Kirk argues in the classic series episode *A Taste of Armageddon*:

> ANAN7: There can be no peace, don't you see, we've admit-ted it to ourselves. We're a killer species, it's instinctive! It's the same with you …
>
> KIRK: All right, it's instinctive, the instinct can be fought. We're human beings with the blood of a million savage years on our hands, but we can stop it! We can admit that we're killers but that we're not going to kill today, that's all it takes, knowing that we're not going to kill … today.[5]

This of course returns us to the Kantian notion of duty and 'ought' referred to back in Chapter Two. The understanding of the human condition that identifies morality with the exercise of the rational will over our baser instincts.

Anakin Skywalker – portrayed within episodes one to three of the Star Wars saga is a different case to the Batman entirely. Here is a person who does indeed become ruled by his memories of one bad day, the day his mother was violently killed and the day he took bloody revenge upon her killers. Anakin's hatred and fear are seen as dominating him to such an extent that he is easily manipulated and corrupted. He falls into all the traps of expedi-ency, use of the weapons of the enemy and the misuse of power that we have previously spoken of.

Fear seems to play a significant part in making Anakin Skywalker susceptible to the baleful influence of the evil emperor and the dark side of the Force and thus catalysing his transformation into the villainous Darth Vader. As we have mentioned in Chapter Two fear of otherness is very much at the heart of the villainous persona. The villain – it would appear – finds it extraordinarily difficult to cope with a complicated world characterised by difference and variety. The desire to impose order and control, to create an empire, is often the primary goal of the villainous mastermind. We see this in a variety of villains from Saruman to Vito Corleone from Darth Vader to Lex Luthor. The uniformity that comes with an empire, with its hierarchy culminating in a supreme ruler, makes it an ideal environment for the villain.

The Doctor's long-time enemy, the Daleks, represent one of the starkest manifestations of the villain as characterised by hatred of otherness and the desire to bring it under control or to destroy it:

> VAN STATTEN: Why not just reason with this Dalek? It must be willing to negotiate, there must be something it needs, everything needs something.
> THE DOCTOR: What's the nearest town?
> VAN STATTEN: Salt Lake City.
> THE DOCTOR: Population?
> VAN STATTEN: One million.
> THE DOCTOR: All dead. If the Dalek gets out it'll murder every living creature, that's all it needs.
> VAN STATTEN: But why would it do that!?
> THE DOCTOR: Because it honestly believes they should die. Human beings are different and anything different is wrong. It's the ultimate in racial cleansing.[6]

It may be something of a cliché but it would seem that in contra distinction to the villainous tendency towards domination and control the hero is characterised by self-giving, even self-abandonment, to the other. The phenomenologist and ethicist Emmanuel Levinas marks out two modes of engagement with the world. The first he refers to as the ontological relationship – characterised by the reduction of difference and otherness to the same, while the second he calls the metaphysical relationship. It is this later relationship that prioritises the other and abandons the notions of power and possession as modes of encounter with the world. This for Levinas is the true basis for an authentic ethical response to the world.

> my duty to respond to the other suspends my natural right to self-survival, *le droit vitale*. My ethical relation of love for the other stems from the fact that the self cannot survive by itself alone, cannot find meaning within its own being-in-the-world, within the ontology of sameness ... To expose myself to the vulnerability of the face *[the initial way in which we encounter the other for Levinas]* is to put my ontological right to exist into question. In ethics, the other's right to exist has primacy over my own, a primacy epitomised in the ethical edict: you shall not kill, you shall not jeopardise the life of the other.[7]

As we have seen, self-sacrifice – often in the face of over-whelming opposition and apparent lack of hope – are the hallmarks of the hero. Whether we are speaking of Jesus of Nazareth, or Buffy, or Harry Potter, or even anti-heroes such as Marv from Frank Miller's *Sin City*, the decision to give up one's life for another, to value another more than oneself, to place oneself between another and harm is, I believe, fundamentally heroic.

On learning that the powerful political figure Patrick Roark was behind the death of the prostitute Goldie the brutal and violently unbalanced Marv – to whom she had shown a degree of kindness – goes looking for revenge:

> Every inch of me wants to turn tail. To sneak into the back of a truck or hop a freight car and haul out of town. I want to run, run like hell, to crawl into a cave somewhere and forget about Goldie and Lucille and silent, deadly Kevin. Roark. Damn it. I'm as good as dead. I'm as good as dead. And its not that I'm any kind of hero that makes me stay. Heroes don't go weak in the knees and feel like throwing up or curling up into a little ball and crying like a baby ... I owe you, Goldie. I owe you and I'm going to pay up. So going

after Roark means dying, win or lose. Hell, dying will be nothing. I'll die laughing if I know I've done this one thing right.[8]

Marv is by no means a traditional hero. His methods for extracting information are harsh and bloody and yet, it is hard not to view him as a hero. Part of this is due, I think, both to his motivation and his willingness to suffer in his quest for vengeance. Marv knows he is out of his depth, he is just one man against an entire corrupt city, he quickly realises that he is unlikely to survive his crusade to punish Goldie's murderers and that he will no doubt die horribly at the hands of powers he cannot defeat simply with his fists. Yet for all that, he continues, he fights, he suffers incredible damage and although he finds and kills Roark he is captured, framed for the murder of Goldie and a number of other women and finally electrocuted to death.

Once again, the hero, it would appear, has less to do with power and ability than with attitude. In the excellent book *Superheroes and Philosophy: Truth Justice and the Socratic Way* Tom and Matt Morris argue that:

> In an interesting way, we can and should extend our concept of the heroic beyond those occupations that obviously require facing personal danger for the good of others, or that involves financial sacrifice in the service of what is socially needed. We should realize that a stay-at-home mother can be a hero, as can a public servant, an engineer, a musician, or an artist. Anyone who stands for the good and the right, and does so against the pull of forces that would defeat their effort can be seen as heroic.[9]

The hero makes themselves available to others at a variety of levels. They share joy and pain, they sympathize and sometimes even empathize with those whom they feel responsible for. They are prepared to be a resource for the other, who may very well be a stranger to them, to such an extent that their emotional and physical energies are the others to draw upon, to lighten the burden of their pain and anguish without any apparent benefit to the hero themselves. To love the other is to forget oneself as a predominant concern, to make oneself totally available to and for the other. It is in this way, in losing ourselves, that we gain heroic stature. In this sense, in giving ourselves over to the other as a resource we also raise the hope that such a resource will be available to us when we need it. This hope is, however always just that – hope, never a claim or demand, the true hero makes no demands on the other. The existentialist thinker Søren Kierkegaard clearly understood this hope of being remembered by love in the act of forgetting self when he wrote:

> … the lover in his love thinks only about giving fearlessness and saving another from death. Yet the lover is not therefore forgotten. No, the one who lovingly forgets himself, forgets his own suffering to consider another's misery, forgets what he himself loves in order lovingly to consider another's loss, forgets his own advantage in order lovingly to look at another's: truly such a one is not forgotten. There is One who considers him: God in heaven; or love considers him … The self-lover is busy, he shrieks and shouts, and stands for his rights in order to make certain of not being forgotten – and yet he is forgotten; but the lover who forgets himself, he is remembered by love.[10]

The hero in many ways represents this hope, the hope that in a world increasingly dominated by fear, mistrust and self-centeredness where otherness and difference are looked upon with suspicion that there is another way. It is this functioning as an alternative social paradigm that the Christian ethicist Stanley Hauerwas has in mind when he talks of the Christian Church as 'a community of character', a 'contrast model' to a world constituted by strangers and dominated by fear.[11] Without an alternate example, a palpable demonstration of the way things could be there is no hope for change. As Jim Gordon says to the Batman with reference to the Joker 'we have to show him that our way works'.

To be heroic may mean nothing more than this then, to stand in the face of the *status quo*, in the face of an easy collapse into the madness of an increasingly chaotic world and represent another way. To be heroic does not have to mean possessing the ability to stand against the evils of the world, either well or successfully, but just that one is willing to stand. In this context Morris and Morris raise the point that the notion of the super-hero might therefore be regarded as incoherent.

> The reasoning is simple. The more powerful a person is, the less he or she would risk in fighting evil or helping someone else. What's so heroic about stopping an armed robbery if your skin is bullet proof and your strength is irresistible by any ordinary, or even extraordinary, street thug?[12]

We hear this argument put forward whenever the very rich give, what by ordinary standards would be considered, a large sum of money to charity. The billionaire who donates thousands to a good cause is not often seen as performing a heroic act: 'Oh that's just peanuts to them – they'll hardly even notice it and anyway it's probably a tax dodge'. The notion of proportionality is clearly an issue here and once again this returns us to the Stan Lee *Spiderman* quote 'with great power comes great responsibility'.[13]

Often the super heroes such as Buffy or Spiderman for example, have to sacrifice an ordinary human life for the sake of their heroic calling. The price they have to pay may not be in blood and physical pain, due to their enhanced abilities, but in social and emotional anguish. How many times has Buffy missed out on a social event or had to lie to her mother in order to fulfil her role as the slayer? How many times has Peter Parker had to stand up Mary Jane because he heard a cry for help that he could not ignore?

The possession of power and ability should no more debar one from heroism than should the lack of those things. For an individual to stand in the path of an oncoming tank, for a corporation to decide that it will only 'trade fairly' in the world market place and for a government to make a commitment to radical environmental policies all of these things could well be considered heroic. These are stands against what maybe convenient and expedient and efficient and cost-effective. Heroes make their choices not on the basis of the powers they may or may not wield, but on the basis of how and when and for whom they may deploy the powers they actually have at their disposal.[14]

Heroism, as we have been suggesting throughout this work,

has to do with abandoning oneself to the other, deploying one's powers in the service of the other, irrespective of personal safety or reward, and irrespective of success or failure.

As Morris and Morris quite rightly observe:

> In a culture of pervasive self-interest and self-indulgent passivity, where people are often more inclined to be spectators than participants, and typically embrace easy comfort rather than initiating needed change, we can forget the relative rarity of the motivation behind what is actually heroic activity.[15]

If being a hero has to do with the giving of oneself and one's abilities and powers over to the wider world then, by the same token, being a villain has to do with the withholding of oneself from that world.

We have spoken of the villain as armouring themselves against the world, seeking to distance themselves from a world that in many ways they seem to fear due to its apparent chaotic complexity. The marginalising or even demonising of a particular individual or group is a common political tool used to render violent and perhaps even unjust action towards others more palatable to the general populous. However, it seems to me that a potentially greater evil arises out of the self-isolation of an individual or group from the rest of the world. To see a certain social or racial group as different from the rest of humanity is a dangerous and potentially bloody thing indeed, yet to see oneself as different from the rest of humanity is, I believe, the basis for true villainy.

One of the reasons that the likes of the cannibalistic psychopath Hannibal Lecter, the cyborg menace the Borg from *Star Trek*, and the Daleks from *Doctor Who* are regarded as so villainous is that they understand themselves as unrelated to anything other than themselves. Thus everything that they encounter is to be regarded as a resource, something that can be consumed and used. The villain is, first and foremost, a user.

Once again it would appear that being a villain has more to do with a particular attitude of mind rather than any particular power, or indeed any particular action. To see the world and those within it as a thing to be made use of, a thing that we are in no way responsible for or even connected to is, in my view, the height of villainy – whether this be witnessed to in the playground, the street, the home, the office or internationally.

Living our lives as we do, behind our eyes and inside our own heads there is an inevitable self-centeredness that characterises our existence. We have to work hard not to see the world as revolving around us because, in a very real and existential sense it actually does. As Kant teaches us, the whole external world is made available to us via representation, not as it is *in-itself*. The world is the world that I experience and that is interpreted by my mind, it takes a great deal of maturity to be able to avoid the arrogance that comes with this realisation. It is for this reason that those in their teens are often accused of not caring or being self-absorbed as they possess many of the freedoms of an adult life yet lack the social maturity to see themselves as part of a complex social web. In short, they lack the necessary sense of responsibility towards the other.

It is no surprise that for many villains the possession of a godlike status is their ultimate goal. To be as a god inevitably marks one out as different from all other beings. Indeed, by definition, and as we mentioned back in Chapter Two, to be divine implies transcendence, that is, being in some way beyond this world. Now of course as we have already mentioned, we all transcend one another to a certain extent. We all exist as others to those around us. As a general rule I would argue that how we overcome this otherness is a source of perpetual anxiety to us. However, we may choose to avoid this permanent state of angst by simply revelling in our transcendence, in our distance from others.

Joseph Campbell makes this point when he discusses the heroic formula where an individual is plucked out of their ordinary life, encounters forces that bestow special powers and abilities upon them and then returns to the ordinary world to use their new powers in the service of others. Campbell argues that this heroic process can be short-circuited, particularly at the point at which the nascent hero is supposed to return and reintegrate with society. The hero may find this return the most difficult requirement of all. For if he has won through, like the Buddha, to the profound repose of complete enlightenment, there is danger that the bliss of this experience may annihilate all recollection of, interest in, or hope for, the sorrows of the world.[16]

To collapse into villainy may only take an overestimation of our own transcendence, a transcendence that actually exists but needs to be constantly overcome. Once again the issue of power and ability comes into play here as the more powerful one is the easier it is to see oneself as special, in someway other than the herd, a superman. Indeed, it is in his adopting of the Clark Kent persona that Superman may be seen to be at his most heroic as he seeks through it to become more closely connected to humanity rather than to use his almost godlike powers to justify remoteness.

In the classic 1966 *Star Trek* episode 'Where No Man Has Gone Before', the theme of absolute power corrupting absolutely is explored. In this story Captain Kirk's long time friend and colleague Gary Mitchell and eventually the psychiatrist Doctor Elizabeth Dehner are accidentally empowered with god-like abilities. As Mitchell becomes more distant from his human friends and crewmates he becomes more callous towards them and more dismissive:

MITCHELL: You'll soon share this feeling Elizabeth, to be like God, to have the power to make the world anything you want it to be.

(Kirk approaches intent on destroying Mitchell – Mitchell senses his presence)

MITCHELL: Go to him Elizabeth, talk to him, now that you're changing I want you to see just how unimportant they are.

(Elizabeth teleports herself to Kirk)

ELIZABETH: Yes, it just took a little longer for it to happen to me … what he is doing is right, for him and for me …

KIRK: … and for humanity? You're still human …

ELIZABETH: No …

KIRK: … at least partly you are! Or you wouldn't be here

talking to me.

ELIZABETH: Earth is really unimportant. Before long we will be where it would have taken mankind millions of years of learning to reach.

KIRK: And what will Mitchell learn in getting there? Will he know what to do with his power? Will he acquire the wisdom? ... Did you hear him joke about compassion? Of all else a god needs compassion!

ELIZABETH: What do you know about gods?

KIRK: Well, lets talk about humans, about our frailties. As powerful as he gets he'll still have all of that inside him ... you know the ugly savage things we all keep buried that none of us dare expose, but he'll dare, who's to stop him? He doesn't need to care![17]

If great power does indeed demand a corresponding level of responsibility then it also appears to be true that power corrupts and that absolute power corrupts absolutely. To believe oneself to be absolutely other than the rest of the world destroys the sense of fellow feeling upon which sympathy and empathy depend. To see ourselves as unconnected to the world – as technologically driven Western culture has tended to – encourages us to use the world, to seek to dominate and manipulate our environment rather than live as part of it. Absence of respect for the environment and the wider animal world can, I believe, be regarded as an act of villainy not simply due to the lack of regard for the non-human world that this reflects, but also because of the lack of empathy with future generations that this exhibits.

One of the reasons that the Doctor chooses to live life as a renegade in space and time, exiled from his people, is precisely because the Time Lords, in spite of their godlike technology, refuse to involve themselves in the affairs of others. While the Doctor sees this remoteness from less technologically developed lifeforms as aloof and morally bankrupt, the Time Lords see it as the only way to allow other races to develop naturally. This returns us to the issue of whether a powerful individual or group has the right to intervene in the affairs of others.

In *Fantastic Four Issue 13* we are introduced to an almost divine race known only as The Watchers who, true to their name have dedicated themselves simply to watch other races and record what they see. As a species they have decided never to interfere in the lives of other races for fear of repeating a cultural accident where their offering of atomic energy to the Proscilicans lead to that species all but wiping themselves out in nuclear war. Having said that, one of their number, Uatu, occasionally went against the Watcher's absolute code of non-interference. One such instance was when the Earth was threatened by another godlike being Galactus.

Galactus needs to consume whole planets to sustain himself and Earth is just another consumable energy source. Uatu comes to the Fantastic Four's aid in the defence of the planet and confronts Galactus:

> GALACTUS: So! Twas you who conspired to hide this paltry world from the eyes of Galactus! Know you not that none may thwart my will?
>
> WATCHER: Heed my words, pillager of the planets! This tiny speck of matter upon which we stand contains intelligent life! You must not destroy it!
>
> GALACTUS: Of what import are brief, nameless lives ... to Galactus? ... It is not my intention to injure any living being! But ... I must replenish my energy! If petty creatures are wiped out when I drain a planet, it is regrettable ... but unavoidable![18]

Galactus does not regard himself as in any sense 'evil' – indeed neither does the Watcher Uatu for that matter – yet his over-whelming power and cosmic perspective engenders in him a profound indifference to other 'lesser' species in spite of the fact that he was originally very much like we are. At a rather more mundane level this could be likened to the person who forgets his workmates on receiving a promotion to management, the soldier who forgets what it is like on the battlefield once they are promoted to a more logistical position and the politician who becomes increasingly uninterested in his or her local constituency.[19]

With this in mind, it should not surprise us to find a strong incarnational motif within a great deal of heroic literature as well as within many of the religions of the world. The notion of incarnation has to do with taking on human flesh and dwelling within the human world. The Christian religion for example has long held that Jesus, far from being simply a good example to follow, is nothing less than God in human form. The Christian notion of incarnation speaks of a God who takes on the human condition – as John's gospel would have it, the Word of God, the creator of all things, the bringer of life and light 'became flesh and lived for a while among us' (John 1:14). The reference to flesh is a deliberate attempt to emphasise that this is no illusion or useful didactic conceit but the supreme being in some mysterious way becoming like us, the ultimate exercise in empathy.

We have already referred to Superman's *alter ego*, the very ordinary Clark Kent. It is as Kent that Kal-El becomes incarnate in the world, establishes his humanity, and prevents himself from becoming a distant and remote figure dwelling in his Fortress of Solitude. Kal-El could remain in his Superman persona, removed from the world, immortal, invulnerable, untouched, he chooses not to.

In the 2005 film retelling of the Batman's origin *Batman Begins*,[20] there is a significant incarnational moment when Bruce Wayne realises that by virtue of his privilege and wealth he is too distant from the needs of ordinary people and also too removed from the criminal mentality. In a symbolic moment Bruce exchanges coats with a street person and disappears for a number of years living on the street amongst those who he hopes to protect and also the criminals he hopes to understand.

In *The Lord of The Rings*, Aragorn – the long-lost king – is introduced as a ranger, a man living rough out in the wilderness and known to everyone as Strider. It is as an ordinary man fighting and suffering with others that Aragorn comes to accept his kingly responsibilities.

Maintaining a sense of connectedness with our world and with those in it is essential to the heroic mind set, indeed I would argue that this is the essential difference between the hero and the villain. To be a hero does not require power or ability or status or recognition or knowledge but simply that one exists fully in and as part of the world. This is something that we learn as we grow and develop social skills but it is equally something we can suppress for all manner of reasons. As we have mentioned, we can choose to embrace difference and otherness giving ourselves over to the other in the knowledge that only through heroic self-giving do we truly discover ourselves or we can choose to armour ourselves against the world.

As I write, the news has just come through of a series of terrorist bombs having been detonated throughout London's public transport system.[21] In a world where such atrocities are committed with depressing regularity it is hard not to view the other as a stranger to be feared and shielded against. The potential for villainy is heightened when we give into fear, when we evacuate public spaces, when we demonise those who are not 'one of our own' when we act in a callous and unfeeling way towards those that we consider a threat. Villainy and heroism may thus be seen as examples of our highest ideals and darkest fears for human existence.[22]

For every hero who dons mask and cape and confronts the ranks of the criminal underworld there are countless heroes who simply choose to get up and go out into the world to encounter what it has to offer. For every hero who wields an enchanted blade to defeat the forces of darkness there are millions who deploy whatever gifts and abilities they might possess in the service of others. For every lone warrior who stands unaided against insurmountable evil there are innumerable individuals who make a stand against corporate and political injustice, not because they think they might win, but because they know it to be right.

Similarly, for every mad scientist who utilises their knowledge in the cause of world domination there are those who choose to use their knowledge, however petty, to dominate and control their friends and family. For every dark lord with pretensions to godhood there are individuals who see themselves as separate from the rest of humanity, as having no kinship with others. For every villain who seeks to enslave the human race or transform it into mindless puppets there is the individual who sees others as simply a resource to be used for work or pleasure.

The hero may simply be the person who stops to help a

stranger pick up some dropped items in the street, the villain may simply be the individual who uses others for sexual gratification.

Every day, and throughout our entire lives we wake, we confront the world and we must ask ourselves: Today, am I hero or villain?[23] This is of course not to say that these are the only two modes of being in the world. We are not always called upon to act heroically – even Superman simply gets on with his job and hangs out with his friends sometimes – nor are we tempted to constant villainy. Heroism and villainy are often only apparent in *extremis*, I doubt that it is possible to eat one's lunch heroically or spring-clean the house in a villainous way. For much of the time we may find that we are not called upon to make a conscious choice about our heroic or villainous way of being in the world. Similarly, there may very well be situations that confront us that are beyond our powers to deal with. Spiderman, for example, could not save his first love from death at the hands of the Green Goblin; the Batman couldn't save Jason Todd – the second Robin – from death; and Superman for all his power cannot be everywhere at once, cannot save everyone all the time.

It seems to me that we are only ever called upon to be heroic within the context of our situation and within the limits of our powers. Our own personal circumstances may very well make it impossible to respond heroically to certain situations – fear of heights, lack of physical strength or education may be as much a hindrance to our ability to act heroically as not being able to fly or control the weather. As we have mentioned, being heroic has more to do with how we use what we have whenever appropriate than it has to do with the deployment of super-powers.

While being a hero, for example, may indeed come down to a matter of choice, failing to make that choice, for whatever reason, does not necessarily establish one as a villain. While everyone may possess the potential for heroism and villainy it must be recognised that almost by definition these are special characteristics that stand out from the norm. Not taking on the armed gunman or returning to a burning building to save a trapped child does not necessarily make us bad or immoral people any more than the occasional lapse in morality would make us villainous monsters. We are human beings with all the strengths and weaknesses of our species. Occasionally we reach the heights of heroic self-sacrifice and at other times we sink down into villainous self-serving. Being aware of the extremes to which we can be drawn is, in my view, one of the most important pieces of self-knowledge we will ever possess.

In the light of all that we have said so far, all the glorious heroic figures we have introduced and all the life or death battles they have fought to protect the world from darkness, perhaps the most that one can ever say about heroes is that they acknowledge their responsibilities and act on them. Often we recognise our obligations to others and the world but lack the strength to act, other times we may possess power and ability but fail to see what needs to be done. The hero, it might be said, is called into being when perception of a need and the recognition of responsibility toward it are backed up by the will to act. For this reason it makes more sense to me to speak of heroism and villainy as ways of being in the world rather than as having to do with innate abilities or powers. For this reason it is possible for any one of us to become heroic or villainous. Furthermore it serves as a reminder to those accustomed to heroism and villainy that they need not be heroes and villains all the time.

Notes

Preface

1. Alsford, M., *What If? Religious Themes in Science Fiction*, DLT, 2000, p.1.
2. Foucault, M., *The Order of Things*, Routledge,1992, p.374.
3. ibid., pp.342–3.

Chapter One: Myth and imagination

1. Campbell, J. *The Hero with a Thousand Faces*, Fontana, 1993 (originally published 1949).
2. ibid., p.23.
3. For more on this see my book *What If?* DLT, 2000, pp.83ff.
4. Aristotle, *Metaphysics, Part 1*, Penguin Classics, 1998.
5. Job 7:29, NIV Bible, Hodder & Stoughton, 1979.
6. ibid., Job 8:20.
7. See Chapter Four, p.110ff., on 'The Beast Within'.
8. The death of a loved one as the motivation is a very common motif for comic heroes such as the Batman, Spiderman and Daredevil for example. Cf. Chapter 5.
9. Cf. Chapter Two for more on 'otherness'.
10. Plato, *The Republic, Book 7.1*, Penguin Classics, 1977, p.261. Cf. http://classics.mit.edu/Plato/republic.html for online version.
11. ibid., p.318.
12. ibid., p.319.
13. The significance of this observation, by arguably the greatest of all the Greek philosophers, has not been lost on those who follow the Christian tradition and parallels between the enlightened cave dweller and the man Jesus have routinely been drawn.
14. Russell, B., *History of Western Philosophy*, George Allen & Unwin Ltd, 1975, p.147.
15. *The Matrix, The Matrix Reloaded, Matrix Revolutions*.
16. Descartes, R., *Second Meditation*, Penguin Classics, 1976, p.103.
17. Descartes, R., *Discourse 2*, Penguin Classics, 1977, p.41
18. Russell, B., *Power, A New Social Analysis*, George Allen & Unwin Ltd, 1938, pp.8–9.

19. Wittgenstein, L. *Tractatus 1 and 7*, Routledge, 2001; cf. http://guava. phil.lehigh.edu/tlp/trac.htm for online version.

20. Derrida, J., *Writing and Difference*, Routledge, 2001, p.7.

21. Cranston, M., *The Romantic Movement*, Blackwell, 1994, p.11.

22. Byron in point of fact held rather a dim view of the capacity of human imagination famously arguing that an Irish peasant with a little whisky could imagine enough to produce a modern poem.

23. Blake, W., *Milton: A Poem*, Thames & Hudson, 1979.

24. Wordsworth, W., 'The Tables Turned', see www.bartleby.com/145/ ww134.html

25. Cf. for example Jean Baudrillard's work on Simulacra particularly in *Simulacra and Simulation*, University of Michigan Press, 1994.

Chapter Two: The Outsider – Heroes and otherness

1. Campbell, J., *The Hero with a Thousand Faces*, Fontana; p.30.

2. Kant of course uses the term transcendental in a rather different way in the *First Critique*: see *The Critique of Pure Reason*, Macmillan, 1982.

3. Cf. Pantheism and Process Theology for example, see God as in some way present in and even as part of the world.

4. Bonhoeffer, D., Letter to Eberhard Bethge, 30 April 1944, found in *Letters and Papers from Prison*, SCM, 2001.

5. Kant, Immanual, *Groundwork of the Metaphysics of Morals*, CUP, 1998, p.113.

6. ibid., p.65.

7. ibid., p.91.

8. ibid.

9. Cassirer, E., Kant's *Life and Thought*, Yale University Press, 1981, p.249.

10. Campbell, p.6.

11. This view is engagingly explored in the novels of Robert Holdstock, principally *Mythago Wood*, Gollancz, 1984.

12. Shelton, J. and Jewett, R., *The Myth of the American Superhero*, Eerdmans, 2002, p.6.

13. Tarantino, Quentin, *Kill Bill Vol.2*, Miramax, 2004.

14. Cf. *Journey into Mystery 87* and *89* for example, Marvel Comics, 1962, 1963.

15. Cf. *The Amazing Spiderman 4* and *5*, Marvel Comics, 1963, for an early example of this but similarly the more contemporary retelling of the Spiderman saga in *The Ultimate Spiderman* series. This aspect of Spiderman's often tortured career can be seen from page one of his very first appearance in *Amazing Fantasy 15* published in August 1962 (Marvel) where a group of teenagers write off the studious Peter Parker as 'Midtown High's only professional wallflower'.

16. *The Amazing Spider-Man*, Marvel Comics, 4 September 1963.

17. *Warrior 3*, Quality Communications, 1982.

18. Nietzsche, F., *Thus Spake Zarathustra*, Wordsworth Classics, Prologue, pt

3, pp.6–7.

19. ibid., Chapter 73, Sections 2 and 3, pp.276–277.
20. *Buffy the Vampire Slayer*, Series Seven, 'Lessons'.
21. *The Empire Strikes Back*, Lucasfilms, 1980.
22. Busiek, Kurt, *Astro City: Life in the Big City*, Homage/DC Comics, 1996, pp.13–14.
23. ibid., pp. 13–35.
24. Campbell, 1993, p.37.
25. Jungel, Eberhard, *Death: the Riddle and the Mystery*, Westminster Press, 1974, p.109.
26. Barth, Karl, *The Christian Life, Church Dogmatics, Vol. IV/4,* Lecture Fragments, trans. G.W. Bromiley, T&T Clark, 1981, p.212.
27. The original story has this happen in Vietnam during the 1960s and Stark being held by an unscrupulous communist tyrant Wong-Chu, however as time and ideologies move on this 'origin story' has come under various revisions distancing Stark from munitions development and the conflict in Vietnam.
28. *Iron Man*, Marvel Comics, Vol.1, No. 193, April 1985.
29. *Fantastic Four Annual 2*, Marvel Comics, p.10, 1964.
30. ibid., p.11.
31. The song I most associate with this burgeoning teenaged angst was Simon & Garfunkel's *I Am A Rock*, taken from the 1966 album *Sounds of Silence.*
32. In Ursula Le Guin's *Earthsea* trilogy (Puffin, 2004), for example, the basis of a sorcerer's power lay in his knowledge of the names of people and things. This idea of power through knowledge of a person's name is common throughout the world's mythologies and legends.
33. Moltmann, J., *God in Creation*, SCM Press, 1985, p.32.
34. Superman, Captain Marvel, Spiderman, Frodo Baggins, Harry Potter, to name but a few.
35. *Batman 47*, DC Comics, 1948.
36. Reynolds, Richard, *Superheroes: A Modern Mythology*, Jackson, 1992, p.12.
37. Batman 47, 1948.
38. It is interesting to note that the Batman resigns from the Justice League of America and eventually forms the Outsiders on a matter of principle which marks him out as totally at odds with Superman's heroic ideals. the Batman wishes to cross a national border to rescue a friend and involve himself in a revolution. The so called Justice League of America – represented by Superman – refuses to act. Batman's response is an impassioned one:

> BATMAN: I've heard the cries of the dying … and the mourning … the victims of injustice … I swore I'd do everything in my power to avenge those deaths … to protect innocent lives … and if I fail to keep that promise … my entire life is a lie!

SUPERMAN: But the three of us … [Superman, Batman and Wonder Woman] we've always served as an example to the others [members of the JLA].

BATMAN: I never asked for that, Superman! I never wanted men to imitate me … only fear me! I only want to do my work!

Batman and The Outsiders 1, 1983

39. Mill, John Stuart, *Utilitarianism*, (1863), OUP, 1998, Chapter 2 (cf. http://www.utilitarianism.com/mill2.htm for online copy).

40. 'A gun is a coward's weapon. A liar's weapon. We kill … too often … because we've made it easy … too easy … sparing ourselves … the mess … and the work'.

Miller, F., Janson, K., Varley, L., *Batman: The Dark Knight Book 3*, DC Comics, 1986, p.45.

41. Miller et al., *Book 2*, DC Comics, 1986, p.12.

42. Cf. Deuteronomy 32:35 Romans 12:19, NIV Bible, Hodder & Stoughton, 1979.

43. A theme explored in R. Mayer, *Super-Folks*, Angus & Robertson, 1978 and also Alan Moore's celebrated *Watchmen*, DC comics, 1986, and in a much lighter vein in the 2004 Pixar film *The Incredibles*.

44. Miller et al., *Book 3*, 1986, p.31, p.35.

45. ibid., *Book 4*, 1986, p.38–40.

46. Pratchett, T., *The Wee Free Men*, Corgi, 2004, p.196.

47. Alsford, M., *What If? Religious Themes in Science Fiction*, DLT, 2000, p.77f.

48. Morris, T. and Morris, M., *Superheroes and Philosophy: Truth Justice and the Socratic Way*, Open Court, 2005, pp.32–33.

49. Ellis, W., *The Authority*, Titan Books, 2000, Book One (collecting issues 1–8), 2000.

50. ibid.

51. Miller, Mark, *Civil War*, Marvel Comics, 2006.

Chapter Three: With great power comes great responsibility

1. Russell, B., *Power, A New Social Analysis*, George Allen & Unwin Ltd, 1938, p.9.

2. ibid., p.35.

3. *It's a Wonderful Life*, Republic Studios, 1946.

4. I clearly have a weak spot for this particular film as I mention it elsewhere. Cf *What If? Religious Themes in Science Fiction*, DLT, 2000, p.24. This theme is also explored in the Season Three *Buffy* episode 'The Wish'

5. Sartre, Jean-Paul, *Being and Nothingness*, Methuen, 1977, p.555–6.

6. cf. Michael Moorcock's *The Eternal Champion* series for a good example of this.

7. Dini, Paul and Ross, Alex, *The World's Greatest Super-Heroes*, DC Comics, 2005.

8. Tolkien, J. R. R., *The Lord of the Rings: The Fellowship of the Ring*, George

Allen & Unwin Ltd, 1969, Chapter 11, 'The Council of Elrond'.

9. Plato, *The Republic*, Introduction, Book 2, pt 1, cf. http://www.constitution.org/pla/republic.htm for online copy.

10. Of course the debate over which is more significant, the universal or the particular, has been an ongoing one since at least the time of Plato and Aristotle.

11. cf. Chapter 2, pp.39–40.

12. cf. especially *Star Wars Episode 3: Revenge of the Sith*.

13. Moorcock, Michael, *Elric of Melniboné*, Anchor Press, 1972, p.175.

14. *Buffy the Vampire Slayer*, Season Three, 'Gingerbread', 1999.

15. Hauerwas, S., *A Community of Character: Towards a Constructive Christian Social Ethic*, Notre Dame, 1981, p.75.

16. Augustine, *The City of God*, Book 22.

17. In the *Summa Theologiae* (*Resources for Christian Living*, US, 1981), Thomas Aquinas cuts this list down to three basic principles – right authority, just cause and right intention. Cf. *Summa Theologiae*, 2a2ae,23–46; see also http://www.ccel.org/a/aquinas/summa/home.html

18. Tolkien, The Fellowship of the Ring, Chapter 11, 'The Council of Elrond'.

19. Murray, R. H., *Individual and State*, Hutchinson & Co, 1946, p.143.

20. ibid., p.144.

21. cf. Karl Popper, *The Open Society and Its Enemies*, vol. 2, Chapter 11–12 Routledge, (1945), 1968, and Bertrand Russell, *A History of Western Philosophy*, Chapter 22, George Allen & Unwin Ltd, 1975.

22. Russell, op.cit., p.712.

23. Hegel, G. W. F., *Logic*, OUP, 1975, p.265.

24. cf. *Philosophy of Right*, Oxford, 1967, cited, F. G. Weiss (ed.), *The Essential Writings*, Harper Torchbooks, 1974, p.299ff.

25. Orwell, George, *Nineteen Eighty-Four*, Penguin, 1972, p.208.

26. Hegel, G. W. F., *The Philosophy of History*, Dover, 1956, p.78ff.

27. Murray, *Individual and State*, p.154.

28. Tolkien, *The Fellowship of the Ring*, Chapter 2, 'The Shadow of the Past'.

29. Pullman, Philip, *Northern Lights*, Scholastic, 1998, p.380.

30. Stevenson, Robert Louis, *The Strange Case of Dr. Jekyll and Mr. Hyde*, 1886; online version http://www.online-literature.com/stevenson/jekyllhyde/10/

31. *Babylon 5*, Season Two, 'Comes the Inquisitor', 1995.

32. *The Authority: Under New Management*, DC Comics, 2000.

33. *The Matrix*, Larry and Andy Wachowski, 1999, cf. http://www.harcon.co.nz/matrix/matrixscript.htm for full script.

34. Campbell, J., *The Hero With a Thousand Faces*, Fontana, 1993, pp.33–34.

35. *Doctor Who*, 'The Face Of Evil',BBC, 1975.

36. Freire, Paulo, The *Pedagogy of the Oppressed*, 1968, (Thirtieth anniversary edition), Continuum, 2000.

37. Freire, The *Pedagogy of the Oppressed*, Chapter 3, cf. online version

http://www.marxists.org/subject/education/freire/pedagogy/
38. Cited G. Wills, *Saint Augustine*, Weidenfeld & Nicolson, 1999, p.103.
39. Smith, Kevin, *Clerks*, Miramax, 1994.

Chapter Four: Villains, monsters and evil masterminds

1. Suskind, R., *The New York Times Magazine*, 17 October 2004, p.44;
   cf. http://www.pastpeak.com/archives/2004/10/the_fuhrer_prin.htm
   for online extracts.
2. It was disconcerting to do an internet search for the Führer principle, so
   as to gather more information on Adolf Hitler, only to have Google
   throw up a significant number of sites relating to George W. Bush.
3. Lukes, S., *Individualism*, Blackwell, 1975, p.7.
4. Moulin, L., 'On the Evolution of the Meaning of the Word
   Individualism', *International Social Science Bulletin*, VII, p.185.
5. Cited S.Lukes, p.27.
6. Emerson, Ralph Waldo, 'Self-Reliance', in *Essays*, 1841 cf.
   http://www.emersoncentral.com/selfreliance.htm
7. De Tocqueville, Alexis, *De la Democratie en Amerique*, Book II, pt 11,
   pp.104–106; cf. http://xroads.virginia.edu/~HYPER/DETOC/ch2_02.htm
8. ibid.
9. *Le Monde*, 2 January, 1969.
10. Tolkien, J. R. R., *The Lord of the Rings: The Fellowship of the Ring*, George
    Allen & Unwin, 1969, Book II, Chapter Six 'Lothlorien', p.366.
11. Lewis, C. S., *The Lion, the Witch and the Wardrobe*, Grafton, 2002, p.25.
12. Orwell, George, *Nineteen Eighty-Four*, Part 3, Chapters 5 and 6, 1949; cf:
    http://www.online-literature.com/orwell/1984/
13. Troeltsch, E., 'The Ideas of Natural Law and Humanity in World Politics'
    1922, in O.Gierke, ed., *Natural Law and the Theory of Society 1500–1800*,
    Beacon Press, 1957, p.204.
14. Nolte, E., *Three Faces of Facism*, Mentor, 1969, pp.554–5.
15. *The Gay Science* 116, cited in *A Nietzsche Reader*, Penguin, 1977, p.102.
16. Nietzsche, Friedrich, *On the Genealogy of Morals*, Second Essay: 'Guilt,
    Bad Conscience and Related Matters', 2. cf. http://www.mala.bc.ca/~
    johnstoi/Nietzsche/genealogytofc.htm for online version.
17. John Locke, *The Second Treatise of Civil Government*, Chapter 2.4, 1690; cf.
    http://www.constitution.org/jl/2ndtreat.htm for online version.
18. ibid., Chapter 2.7.
19. Cf. Hermann Goering, for example, is recorded to have said at his trial,
    'We had orders to obey the head of state. We weren't a band of
    criminals meeting in the woods in the dead of night to plan mass
    murders … The four real conspirators are missing: The Führer,
    Himmler, Bormann, and Goebbels'.
    http://www.law.umkc.edu/faculty/projects/ftrials/nuremberg/
    meetthedefendants.html

20. Hohne, H., *The Order of the Death's Head* (English trans.), Pan, 1969, p.72.

21. Nolte, E. pp.520–21.

22. Trevor-Roper, H., ed. *Hitler's Table Talk 1941–1944*, London, 1953.

23. *Doctor Who*, 'The Evil of the Daleks', episode 2, BBC, original broadcast May 1967.

24. Rowling, J. K., *Harry Potter and the Philosopher's Stone*, Bloomsbury, 1997, p.211.

25. *Doctor Who*, 'Genesis of the Daleks', BBC, original broadcast April 1975.

26. Shakespeare, William, *Macbeth*, Penguin, 1994, Act 4, Scene 1; also http://library.thinkquest.org/2888

27. A similar point is made at the end of Chapter 2 of this book.

28. Lombroso, Cesare, *L'Uomo Delinquente* (Criminal Man), 1876.

29. Cf. Chapter 3.

30. Tolkien, *The Fellowship of the Ring*, Book II, Chapter 10, 'The Breaking of the Fellowship'.

31. Genesis 3:12–13, NIV Bible, Hodder & Stoughton, 1979

32. This is a motif that we see clearly portrayed in the 1956 science fiction film *Forbidden Planet*.

33. Plato, *The Republic*, 9.571c, Penguin Classics, 1974; cf. http://classics.mit.edu/Plato/Republic.html

34. Kant, Immanual, *Lectures on Ethics*, Methuen, 1979, p.164.

35. Nietzsche, Friedrich, *Thus Spake Zarathustra*, Algora Publishing, 2003, pt 1, 'The Three Metamorphoses'.

36. Cf. *The Wolfman* (1941), *Company of Wolves* (1984), *Cat People* (1942; 1982), *American Werewolf in London* (1981), *Ginger Snaps* (2000) and *Dog Soldiers* (2002) for example.

37. Cf. http://www.artchive.com/artchive/G/goya/goya_sleep_of_reason.jpg.html
It should be noted that it has been argued that the etching could be interpreted as suggesting that reason itself is nothing but a dream.

38. In both the *Aliens* and *Jurassic Park* film franchises the theme of over-confidence in reason and its technological tools is very much in evidence.

39. Stoker, Bram, *Dracula*, 1897; cf. http://www.online-literature.com/stoker/dracula/

40. ibid., Chapter 4.

41. Davis, A. and Neary, P., *Wolverine: Bloodlust*, Marvel Comics, 1990.

42. Loeb, J., Lee, J., Williams, S., *Batman: Hush*, Vol. 1, DC Comics, 2003.

43. Pannenberg, Wolfhart, *Anthropology in Theological Perspective*, T&T Clark, 1985, pp.106–7.

44. Conrad, Joseph, *The Secret Agent*, 1907, Chapter 4; http://conrad.thefreelibrary.com

45. Nietzsche, Friedrich, *Beyond Good and Evil*, 146, 1885; cf. http://www.mala.bc.ca/~johnstoi/Nietzsche/beyondgoodandevil_tofc.htm

Chapter Five: Conclusion

1. *Casablanca*, Warner Brothers, 1942.
2. Moore, Alan, Bolland, Brian, Higgins, John, *Batman: The Killing Joke*, DC Comics, 1988.
3. ibid.
4. Reynolds, R., *Super Heroes: A Modern Mythology*, University Press of Mississippi, 1992, p.67.
5. *Star Trek (The Original Series)*, 'A Taste of Armageddon', Paramount, 1967.
6. *Doctor Who, Dalek* (series), BBC, 2005.
7. Kearney, R., *Dialogues with Contemporary Continental Thinkers*, MUP, 1984, p.60.
8. Miller, Frank, *Sin City Vol. 1: The Hard Goodbye*, Dark Horse Books, 2005, pp.131–133 (cf. also the 2005 film (Miramax 2005) of the same name which is an almost exact translation of the comic to film).
9. Morris, T. and Morris, Matt, *Superheroes and Philosophy: Truth Justice and the Socratic Way*, Open Court, 2005, p.14.
10. Kierkegaard, Søren, *The Works of Love*, cited in *A Kierkegaard Anthology*, ed. R. Bretall, Princeton, 1946, p.307.
11. Cf. Hauerwas, S., *A Community of Character: Towards a Constructive Christian Social Ethic*, Notre Dame, 1981.
12. Morris and Morris, p.12.
13. It is interesting to note here that in 2004 Marvel Comics introduced a new comic series, *Powerless*, where they explore what it means to be a hero by re-imaging some of their most significant superheroes, such as Spiderman as ordinary humans without extraordinary powers or abilities. Cf. http://www.marvel.com/catalog/listing.htm?writer= Matt%20Cherniss
14. The comedy super hero film *Mystery Men* (1999) explores this theme through the story of a group of misfit would-be super heroes who end up saving the day through heroic determination rather than any actual super powers.
15. Morris and Morris, p.13.
16. Joseph Campbell, *The Hero with a Thousand Faces*, Fontana, 1993, p.36.
17. *Star Trek (The Original Series)*, 'Where No Man Has Gone Before', 1966.
18. *Fantastic Four Issues 13* and *48*, Marvel Comics, 1966.
19. This theme is explored to great effect in Alan Moore and Dave Gibbons' classic comic mini-series *Watchmen* (DC Comics, 1986) with the character of Doctor Manhattan.
20. *Batman Begins*, Warner Bros, 2005.
21. 7 July 2005.
22. It is recognised of course that the notion of hero and villain may very well be culturally or ideologically relative – for example there were 'Heroes of the Third Reich' who embodied the ideals of that particular

world view. While at one level the notion of hero is still partially intact here – an orientation towards the community as a whole, self-sacrifice for a higher cause and so on – I would suggest that hero's basic essence is compromised by an allegiance to any ideology that marginalises, demonises or promotes any form of totalitarianism. Such ideologies demonstrate both an abuse of power and an exaggerated sense of transcendence such as we have associated with the notion of villainy throughout this work.

23. Mike Mignola's comic character *Hellboy* is a good example of a hero who while being essentially a demon is portrayed as overcoming his nature and fighting for good through the exercise of his will and through the influence of his upbringing. Cf. *Hellboy: Seed of Destruction*, Dark Horse Books, 1994, also the 2004 Columbia Tristar film adaptation *Hellboy*.

Further Reading and Viewing

(All publishing details and dates refer to the texts used by the author and do not necessarily reflect original dates of publication.)

M. Alsford, *What If? Religious Themes in Science Fiction*, DLT, 2000

Aristotle, *Metaphysics*, Penguin Classics, 1998

Barth, K., *The Christian Life, Church Dogmatics*, Vol. IV/4, Lecture Fragments, trans. G.W.Bromiley, T. & T. Clark, 1981

Baudrillard, J., *Simulacra and Simulation*, Michigan, 1994

Campbell, J., *The Hero with a Thousand Faces*, Fontana, 1993 (originally published 1949)

Cassirer, E., Kant's *Life and Thought*, Yale University Press, 1981

Conroy, M., *Comicbook Action Heroes*, Chrysalis, 2002

Cranston, M., *The Romantic Movement*, Blackwell, 1994

Derrida, J., *Writing & Difference*, Routledge, 1993

Descartes, R., *Discourse on Method and Other Writings*, Penguin Classics, 1976

Emerson, Ralph Waldo, *Self-Reliance*, in *Essays*, 1841; see http://www.emersoncentral.com/selfreliance.htm

Fingeroth, D., *Superman on the Couch*, Continuum, 2004

Freire, Paulo, The *Pedagogy of the Oppressed*, 1968 (Thirtieth anniversary edition) Continuum, 2000

Hauerwas, S., *A Community of Character: Towards a Constructive Christian Social Ethic*, Notre Dame, 1981

Hohne, H., *The Order of the Death's Head*, (English trans.) Pan, 1969

Holdstock, R., *Mythago Wood*, Gollancz, 1984

Horn, M., *The World Encyclopedia of Comics*, Chelsea House, 1999

Jungel, E., *Death; the Riddle and the Mystery*, Westminster Press, 1974

Kant, Immanuel, *Groundwork of the Metaphysics of Morals*, CUP, 1998

Kearney, R., *Dialogues with Contemporary Continental Thinkers*, MUP, 1984

Kierkegaard, Søren, *The Works of Love*, cited in *A Kierkegaard Anthology*, ed. R. Bretall, Princeton, 1946

Klock, G., *How to Read Superhero Comics and Why*, Continuum, 2002

Le Guin, Ursula K. *The Earthsea Quartet*, Puffin, 2004

Locke, J., *The Second Treatise of Civil Government*, (1690) CUP, 1988

Lombroso, Cesare, *L'Uomo Delinquente* (Criminal Man), Horpli, 1876

Lukes, S., *Individualism*, Blackwell, 1975

Magnussen, A. and Christiansen, Hans-Christian, *Comics and Culture: Analytical and Theoretical Approaches to Comics*, Museum Tusculanum Press, 2000

Mayer, R., *Super-Folks*, Angus & Robertson, 1978

Mill, John Stuart, *Utilitarianism* (1863), OUP, 1998

Millar, Mark, *Civil War*, Part 1. Marvel Publishing, 2006

Moltmann, J., *God in Creation*, SCM, 1985

Moorcock, M., *Elric of Melniboné*, Anchor Press, 1972

Morris, T. and Morris, Matt, *Superheroes and Philosophy: Truth, Justice and the Socratic Way*, Open Court, 2005

Moulin, L., 'On the Evolution of the Meaning of the Word Individualism', *International Social Science Bulletin*, VII, p.185

Murray, R. H., *Individual and State*, London, Hutchinson & Co., 1946

Nietzsche, F., *On the Genealogy of Morals*, (1887), Dover Publications, 2003

Nietzsche, F., *Thus Spake Zarathustra*, Wordsworth Classics, 1997

Nietzsche, F., *Beyond Good and Evil*, (1885), Dover Publications, 1998

Nietzsche, F., *The Gay Science*, (1882), Random House, 1974

Nolte, E., *Three Faces of Facism*, Mentor, 1969

Plato, *The Republic*, Penguin Classics, 1974

Popper, K., *The Open Society and Its Enemies Vol.2*, (1945), Routledge, 1968

Pratchett, Terry, *The Wee Free Men*, Corgi, 2004

Pullman, Philip, *Northern Lights*, Scholastic, 1998

Reynolds, R., *Superheroes: A Modern Mythology*, Jackson, 1992

Rowling, J. K., *Harry Potter and the Philosopher's Stone*, Bloomsbury, 1997

Russell, B., *Power, A New Social Analysis*, George Allen & Unwin Ltd, 1938

Russell, B., *A history of Western Philosophy*, George Allen & Unwin Ltd, 1975

Sabin, R., *Comics, Comix and Graphic Novels: A History of Comic Art*, Phaidon, 1996

Sartre, Jean-Paul, *Being and Nothingness*, Methuen, 1977

Shelton, J. and Jewett, R., *The Myth of the American Superhero*, Eerdmans, 2002

Simpson, P., Rodiss, H., Bushell. M., (eds) *The Rough Guide To Superheroes*, Rough Guides, 2004

South, J. (ed) *Buffy the Vampire Slayer and Philosophy: Fear and Trembling in Sunnydale*, Open Court, 2003

Stevenson, Robert Louis, *The Strange Case of Dr Jekyll and Mr Hyde*, (1886), Penguin Classics, 2003

Stoker, Bram, *Dracula*, 1897

Tolkien, J. R. R., *The Lord of the Rings*, George Allen & Unwin Ltd, 1969

Trevor-Roper, H. (ed.), *Hitler's Table Talk 1941–1944*, London, 1953

Troeltsch, E., 'The Ideas of Natural Law and Humanity in World Politics' 1922, in O. Gierke, ed., *Natural Law and the Theory of Society 1500–1800*, Beacon Press, 1957

Wills, G., *Saint Augustine*, Weidenfeld & Nicolson, 1999

Wittgenstein, L., *Tractatus*, Routledge, 2001
Wright, N., *The Classic Era of American Comics*, Prion, 2000

Film and television

Casablanca, Warner Brothers, 1942
It's a Wonderful Life, Republic Studios, 1946
Star Trek (The Original Series), 'Where No Man Has Gone Before', Paramount 1966
Star Trek (The Original Series), 'A Taste of Armageddon', Paramount, 1967
Doctor Who, The Face Of Evil (series), BBC, 1975
Doctor Who, Genesis of the Daleks (series), BBC, 1975
The Empire Strikes Back, G. Lucas, 1980
Xena: Warrior Princess, Warner Brothers, 1995–2001
Mystery Men, Universal, 1999
The Matrix, Warner Brothers, 1999
The Matrix Reloaded, Warner Brothers, 2003
Matrix Revolutions, Warner Brothers, 2003
Buffy the Vampire Slayer, Twentieth–Century Fox, 1997–2003
Smallville, Warner Brothers, 2001 ongoing to-date
Kill Bill Vol.2., Miramax, 2004
The Incredibles, Pixar, 2004
Hellboy, Columbia Tristar, 2004
Doctor Who, Dalek (series), BBC, 2005
Batman Begins, Warner Brothers, 2005
Fantastic Four, Twentieth Century Fox, 2005

Comics

There is a wealth of comic and graphic novel material available right now. Most of it is only available from specialist comic shops such as *Forbidden Planet*. Here is just a very small sample of the material I've drawn on for this book.

Batman 47, DC Comics, 1948
Journey into Mystery 87 and *89*, Marvel Comics, 1962 and 1963
Amazing Fantasy 15, Marvel Comics, August 1962
The Amazing Spider-Man 4, Marvel Comics, September 1963
Fantastic Four Annual 2, Marvel Comics, 1964
Fantastic Four 48, Marvel Comics, 1966
Warrior, Quality Communications, 1982
Batman and The Outsiders 1, DC Comics, 1983
Iron Man Vol.1, No 193, Marvel Comics, April 1985

Miller, Frank, Janson, Klaus, Varley, Lynn, *Batman: The Dark Knight*, DC Comics, 1986

Moore, Alan and Gibbons, Dave, *Watchmen*, DC Comics, 1986

Moore, Alan, Bolland, Brian, Higgins, John, *Batman: The Killing Joke* DC Comics, 1988

Davis, A. and Neary, P. *Wolverine: Bloodlust*, Marvel Comics, 1990

Mignola, Mike, *Hellboy: Seed of Destruction*, Dark Horse Books, 1994

Busiek, Kurt, *Astro City: Life in the Big City*, DC Comics, 1999

Ellis, W., Hitch, B., Neary, P., *The Authority: Relentless*, Titan Books, 2000 (collecting issues 1–8)

Moore, Alan, Ha, Gene, Cannon, Zander, *Top 10: Book 1*, America's Best Comics, 2000

Millar, Mark, Hitch, Brian, *The Ultimates: Super-Human*, Marvel Comics, 2002

Loeb, J., Lee, J., Williams, S., *Batman: Hush*, Vol. 1, DC Comics, 2003

Miller, Frank, *Sin City Vol. 1: The Hard Goodbye*, Dark Horse Books, 2005

Dini, Paul and Ross, Alex, *The World's Greatest Super-Heroes*, DC Comics, 2005

Many of the classic superhero tales of the 1960s can be found in cheap reprint form such as the Marvels 'Essential' series such *The Essential Spiderman*. This is an excellent way of filling in some of the early history of these iconic heroes.

Index of Selected Thinkers and Authors

Index of Selected Heroes and Villains

Index of Selected Themes and Subjects